THE Away LEG

THE
Away
LEG

XI FOOTBALL STORIES
FROM ON THE ROAD

Steve Menary
& James Montague

First published by Pitch Publishing, 2021

Pitch Publishing
A2 Yeoman Gate
Yeoman Way
Worthing
Sussex
BN13 3QZ
www.pitchpublishing.co.uk
info@pitchpublishing.co.uk

ISBN 978 1 78531 987 7

Typesetting and origination by Pitch Publishing
Printed and bound in India by Replika Press Pvt. Ltd.

Contents

Foreword

As coronavirus inveigled its corrosive way across the world in the spring of 2020, football – like so many other parts of everyday life – changed irrevocably. When lockdown eased and matches resumed, football became a vicarious activity watched on screens, and the idea of going to a match, home or away, had become a near but intangible memory. The walk to the stadium. The smell of food wafting across open grills. The controlled anarchy of people and police and anticipation were all experiences that were so familiar, yet suddenly so far away.

As the pandemic ate away at simple pleasures like going to a football match that we all once took for granted, a wider and greater sense of community began to emerge. The idea of making a contribution, of helping out for the greater good, seemed important. There isn't really much football writers could offer. But one thing we could try to do is take you back to a different time. To produce an account of the memorable games, of matches big or small. And to do so to help part of society that was creaking under the strain of lack of investment during the worst of the pandemic: social care.

A team of 11 writers – the number seemed appropriate given the subject – would produce accounts of matches from around the world that had stayed with them. In some, the matches and results would be important; others told a larger story. From World Cups and major club finals, from Brazil to Iceland to North Korea, from big crowds and crazy fans to obscure matches and isolated countries, each writer contributed a chapter about games and trips that resonated long after the final whistle.

From personal highlights to notable games and matches that tell a larger story about football in that country, these 11 tales take fans to new places – both fantastical and familiar – and help satisfy that longing for the most human of experiences: going away to the match.

Thanks goes to the writers that joined in helping create *The Away Leg*, to David Goldblatt for his introduction and to Pitch Publishing for taking on an idea that will help Community Integrated Care continue to provide vital social care services at a time that they are needed more than ever.

Steve Menary, New Forest, November 2020

About Community Integrated Care

Community Integrated Care has pioneered inclusive social care for more than three decades. Founded in 1988, it helped to lead the Care in the Community Agenda – supporting the first person with a complex learning disability to secure their own tenancy in Britain.

From these proud origins, the charity has grown to become one of the UK's largest social care providers. It supports around 4,000 people who have learning disabilities, autism, mental health concerns and dementia, working from the Highlands of Scotland to Hampshire in England.

Community Integrated Care is committed to not only providing high-quality care services but to also helping to create a more inclusive society. It has developed a range of award-winning partnerships with major sports and cultural organisations, led national campaigns to build and change attitudes and understanding, and is lobbying for better respect and support for the social care sector and its frontline heroes.

It has been recognised with a range of national honours for its impact and innovation, including being named as the 2019/20 *Charity Times* Charity of the Year.

Introduction
by David Goldblatt

The Away Leg begins with Harry Pearson opening 'a grey box file with a red-and-white sticker advertising the Argentinean newspaper *El Grafico*'. Inside are the relics of his trip to the 1998 World Cup in France, and it carries the odour of 'aged paper' and 'the scent of garlic and black tobacco'. I have a few boxes like that, objects and papers which evoke the sounds and smells of my own away games: the smell of burning bucket seats in Belgrade as the Partizan fans burnt their own stand while their team lost to rivals Red Star; the insistent pulse of a honed 12-piece Ghanaian horn section accompanying their team Asante Kotoko; a tear gas-impregnated face mask from a day in Belo Horizonte, when I attended a protest march, Brazil v Uruguay and a post-match riot all in one day.

Sharply as these moments are etched in my memory, I can barely remember the scores of those games, let alone a passage of play. I'm not alone. As many of the contributors reveal, our memories of football are not straightforward, not least because so little of what we remember is the football being played. In 'The Democratic People's Republic of FIFAland', Harry Pearson's account of the politically charged Iran v USA game at the 1998 World Cup, he finds that most of the near 20 games he went to have been reduced to no more than a handful of split-second sporting moments. More acutely, he reveals how our televisual memories of a match have already been edited before we see them; his match report features a game-long battle between Iranian protestors and the French police that was invisible on the world's screens.

Sometimes we remember even less than those singular moments. In Catherine Etoe's 'One Nil to the Arsenal', her account of the club's historic victory in the 2007 UEFA Women's Cup, she admits that in the second leg, 'I honestly can not remember the finer details of the 90 minutes that followed, I just know that I held my breath for longer than was probably healthy.' Yet, her memory for a detail, seen before the first leg in Umeå in northern Sweden, is precise and poignant, 'A red bike stood propped against the main stand, a baby buggy hugged the front of a blue coffee kiosk.'

Andrew Downie, reporting from São Paulo, Brazil in 'Heavy Metal Futebol', recalls a joyful afternoon at a Portuguesa game in which his only memory is the heap of peanuts he and an old friend shelled on the terraces: a stark contrast to his time at Corinthians' Copa Libertadores fixture with River Plate which descended into furious, theatrical, maniacal violence. Not every match is as brutal and chaotic as that, but there is plenty of maniacal energy and behaviour to distract from the game in hand.

In 'Soldiers Without Weapons', James Corbett went to Ramallah to see Palestine's first competitive home fixture, a moment of huge political and emotional significance. Caught in a crush as ticketless fans stormed the stadium, the mayhem that the game can generate is palpable. In 'The Final Final' Martino Simcik Arese recalls and relishes three mad weeks in Buenos Aires in which the mania envelops the whole city before, during and after games, cancelled matches and postponed dates in the ill-fated 2018 Copa Libertadores Final between River Plate and Boca Juniors.

Sometimes it is not the play, the feints and dribbles, but just the brutal energies and antagonisms of football players that stay with us. No one can remember a damn thing about the football in Chile v Italy at the 1962 World Cup, but we do recall the left hook thrown by Leonel Sánchez at Italian right-back Mario David. It may not have been quite the brawl that was the Battle of Santiago, but Molly Hudson's account of 'The Battle of Valenciennes' takes us back to Cameroon v England at the Women's World Cup 2019, and its explosive emotional atmosphere and sometimes crude rough-housery.

Sometimes we vicariously surf these extraordinary waves of collective energy; sometimes we taste their toxic qualities and it makes us stop and think: what the hell are we doing here? In 'Saturday Night Lights', Arik Rosenstein reports on a game between Beitar Jerusalem and Bnei Sakhnin, the Israeli footballing tribunes of right-wing Zionism and the country's Arab minority. Born and raised in the United States, but long attached through family to Beitar, he finally makes it into Teddy Stadium in Jerusalem and finds himself appalled by the hatred expressed by Beitar's fans.

What keeps us coming back? Just occasionally one is there to taste the ecstasy of winning, of achieving the unbelievable, of just being together when it happens; the celebrations that stay with you longer than the goal that brought them about. In 'I've Come Home', Nick Ames captures one of those moments, when Iceland beat Kosovo in Reykjavík in 2017, and for the first time, miraculously this island of just 330,000 people qualified for the World Cup. Most of them were there to celebrate.

Ecstasy is all very well, but there is a lot more defeat, ennui and even despair in football. In 'The Georgian Crossroads', Steve Menary travelled to the Caucasus to see Dinamo Tbilisi play Lokomotiv Tbilisi, and finds something closer to a wake than a celebration: a ritual suffused with the memory of the great days of Georgian football, when, as part of the Soviet Union, Dinamo Tbilisi could win a European title, but today are both impoverished and unloved.

Football matches as sites of remembrance, or as ludic markers of social change and political conflict, are the themes of our two other contributors. In 'Statuesque', Samindra Kunti sets Feyenoord's victory in the 2002 UEFA Cup Final in the context of the assassination of Pim Fortuyn – Rotterdam's flamboyant right-wing populist politician – and the club and the city's post-industrial decline. In 'Pay No Attention to That Man Behind the Curtain', James Montague's report on the Asian Cup qualifying matches between the DPRK, aka North Korea, and Lebanon has so much political context at both ends of the tie, it's a wonder he could see any football let alone remember it.

Of course, all our correspondents saw and reported on great goals, ugly tackles, and sharp shifts of form and fortune. Yet they are all constantly drawn to the stories and memories of the people making it happen, to the game's place in the wider world, the game's place in their own world, and the strange connection it makes between them.

In the midst of Palestine v Thailand, James Corbett is suddenly connected to his late Everton-supporting grandfather who first took him to a match, and who, as a British soldier serving in the Mandate, was the last member of his family to go to Palestine. In the throwaway line of all time, Harry Pearson tells us that Iran's coach at the World Cup had, prior to his appointment, been running a vegan restaurant in Silicon Valley.

The profound and the trivial, the sublime and ridiculous, the macrocosm and the micros, the personal and the political are all on show at the football, and much of the time that's what we take away and put in our memory boxes; the authors of *The Away Leg* have been generous enough to open theirs and share them with us.

David Goldblatt, Bristol, December 2020

The Democratic People's Republic of FIFAland

by Harry Pearson

USA v Iran
World Cup finals
Lyon, France
21 June 1998

Every so often, when searching for something in the attic, I come across a grey box file with a red-and-white sticker advertising the Argentinean newspaper *El Grafico* stuck on the lid. Occasionally I open it and glance inside. Last weekend for the first time in many years I brought it down the ladder. It's sitting on my desk as I type this: dusty, giving off a musty smell of aged paper tinged – though perhaps I'm imagining this – with the scent of garlic and black tobacco.

Inside are the relics of my trip to the 1998 World Cup – my laminated press pass, a raft of team sheets and tickets, a typed itinerary with hotel phone numbers, the articles I wrote for *The Guardian*, which my mother proudly cut out and kept, and the little booklet I did for *When Saturday Comes*. There is my notebook too, a hardback Black n' Red A5 with a sticker for Urawa Red Diamonds of the J League on the cover. Whenever I see it I smile at the memory of the people who gave it to me – three giggling Japanese women, dressed as Geishas, I'd helped get a taxi to the Stadium Municipal in Toulouse on the day their nation played their first-ever game in a World Cup finals (they were gubbed 6-0).

France 98 was the first time I went to football as a journalist rather than a fan. I spent most of the first week sitting in media centres and on the *tribune de presse* convinced that at some point police would arrest me as an imposter. Later, when I mentioned this to a football writer from the *Daily Express*, he said, 'I feel exactly the same way and I've been doing this for ten years.'

I had a heavy schedule of matches – 17 in 19 days. I criss-crossed the country by train using my Eurorail pass so often I had to get a supplementary booklet to write the journeys in. I stayed in cheap hotels I'd found in the *Le Routard* guide. Some of them were charming, others were so like old people's homes you half expected to find a mug with false teeth in it next to the bed. One night I was in Nantes, the next in Montpelier, the following one in Bordeaux. I travelled over 5,000 miles by rail in three weeks. Not that it was a chore. After all, I was in France, I was watching football and I was getting paid for it.

By the time I'd watched my tenth game, Spain v Paraguay in St Étienne, the matches had started to blur into one. Shaking my memory now I recall Roberto Baggio's equalising penalty in the rain at Stade Lescure, Bordeaux; Cuauhtémoc Blanco's bunny hop in Lyon; a mad refereeing display in Toulouse (South Africa v Denmark) by a Colombian named Rendon; Hristo Stoichkov stomping about like Alexei Sayle imitating Mussolini. The football was often dull, but meeting fans from all nations on trains and buses, hanging around in brasseries with journalists, queuing up at the press-centre cafe for croque monsieur between Bernd Schuster (who was dressed like he was auditioning for the Don Johnson role in *Miami Vice*) and Rinus Michels (who wasn't), it was fabulous. In fact, it was one of the happiest times of my life.

Game number 11 was a Group F fixture at the elegant Stade de Gerland in Lyon. I'd put my name down for a press ticket with limited expectation of getting one. Press passes for matches were allocated by a complex system (nowadays it would be an algorithm, back then it was likely some FIFA official in a blazer with a flow chart, or maybe a blindfold, a list of names and a pin) and since this had been described by one of the competing nation's officials as 'the mother of all games' it seemed likely to me it would be over-subscribed.

Group F was the draw FIFA didn't want and the one most supporters had a feeling was inevitable. At the ceremony in Paris, Germany and the Federal Republic of Yugoslavia (as the agglomeration of Serbia and Montenegro was briefly called) had already been drawn, and they were then joined by the team from Pot C, Iran. Pot D was drawn next. An excited buzz went up when the name was read out: the USA.

Relations between the USA and Iran had been hostile since the revolution of 1979. There had been the hostage crisis of Jimmy Carter's final year as president, and US support for Saddam Hussein when he invaded Iran in 1980. There had been the kidnapping of US citizens in Lebanon by Iranian-sponsored terrorists followed by a bomb attack on the American embassy in Beirut as well as a US barracks. Almost 400 people were killed. In 1988, the US had attacked Iranian oil platforms in the Persian Gulf and shot down an Iranian airliner, killing 290 men, women and children.

In 1993 Bill Clinton placed an embargo on all US trade with Iran.

Sport had inevitably become mixed up in the dispute. When Iranian wrestler Rasoul Khadem won an Olympic medal in Atlanta in 1996, Iran's president Akbar Rafsanjani said the grappler had raised Iran's flag 'in the house of Satan'.

After the draw, US State Department spokesman James Foley took a different tack, suggesting the game might help thaw relations between the two countries: 'If this soccer match is a sign of our ability to deal with each other at least in this one area in a civilised and positive way, that's something we could applaud.'

Iranian officials seemed to be playing down the match as some kind of war minus the bullets, too. 'Governments are one thing,' one said. 'We are friends of the American people.'

US Soccer Federation president Alan Rothenberg, meanwhile, tried to lighten things up with a wisecrack. 'All we need now is an Iraqi referee,' he said. As it was, when an official was allocated for the fixture in Lyon they got the Swiss Urs Meier, who six years later would have to go into hiding after being hounded by irate England fans.

On the face of it the Americans seemed to have the better side, or at least the better known. Their regular starting XI featured several players with experience in the Bundesliga, including captain Thomas Dooley (probably the only player to produce a joke about the 1950s US folk band The Kingston Trio on BBC TV commentary; their most famous single was called 'Hang Down Your Head Tom Dooley' – Chris Waddle the culprit), as well as Premier League goalkeeper Kasey Keller and the ageing but skilful Roy Wegerle, the South African-born striker who had hit 29 goals in 65 starts for QPR a few years earlier. Wegerle was partnered up front by Brian McBride, a big, robust old-school centre-forward who looked like the ranch foreman in a Saturday night western. McBride was said to be on the radar of many English clubs (he would later play 140 games for Fulham and was so popular with the fans they named a bar at Craven Cottage after him) as was midfielder Joe-Max Moore who would end up at Goodison Park.

By comparison the Iran players were largely unknown. The exception was the powerful forward Ali Daei, who'd had such a successful season at Arminia Bielefeld that Bayern Munich had signed him. Those who'd followed the qualification tournament would likely also have recognised the name of his strike partner Khodadad Azizi. Iran had made it through to France via a play-off with Australia. The Aussies, managed by the English media's favourite geezer, Terry Venables, had drawn the first leg in Tehran and been 2-0 up in the second in front of 85,000 fans at Melbourne Cricket Ground. But Iran had clawed their way back and in the 79th minute Azizi – who played for Cologne – had hit the equaliser. Iran sneaked through on away goals, the Australian TV commentators so distraught by the turn of events that one of them broke down in tears. Iran had been underestimated by the Australians, even though several of the team were playing at a good level in Germany. At the MCG they showed they were also tough and resilient.

Despite success in the qualifiers, the Iran FA had lost patience with their Brazilian manager Valdeir Vieira and fired him shortly afterwards. His replacement, the Croatian Tomislav Ivić, had won league titles in seven different countries. He lasted only a few months in Tehran. In came Jalal Talebi, an Iranian who was – ironically – living with his family in the US when he was appointed. Talebi and his wife ran a vegan restaurant in Silicon Valley and he coached part-time in a local college.

Not that there's any mention of that feature of Talebi's life in the printout from the Football Federation Islamic Republic of Iran that was handed to journalists before the game and which I found in my box file.

This told us that as a player Talebi 'demonstrated his outstanding skill during the 1964 preliminary Olympic games in a match between Iran and India'; that as a coach he 'underwent formal and on location training with Chelsea club (14 months), Arsenal club (four months) and with Tottenham club (four months)' and that, in 1996, he was senior advisor to the 'National Indonesian Football Federation'.

None of which quite explained how he came to coach his national team. The fact that he hadn't been appointed until 20 May, three weeks before the tournament started, spoke of panic. However, it quickly became apparent that not only was Talebi a very competent coach he was also a thoroughly decent human being.

His side's opening match in Saint-Étienne ended in a narrow defeat to the talented if politically fragile FR Yugoslavia team. The game's only goal, a direct free kick from the perpetually simmering midfield stomper Siniša Mihajlović, didn't come until the 73rd minute.

The USA had more stability than Iran – coach Steve Sampson had been in charge of the team since 1995. A disciplinarian in the tradition of US gridiron, Sampson had established his authority early on, kicking out skipper John Harkes for complaining about the position he was playing in and other unspecified misdemeanours. He had brought in US players from the European leagues to bolster the inexperienced MLS recruits and managed a creditable runners-up spot in the 1998 Gold Cup, a run that included a 1-0 win over Brazil. The USA cruised through the CONCACAF qualifiers, but a Germany side who were rapidly tilting from 'experienced' to 'past it' easily brushed them aside in their tournament opener – goals from 31-year-old Andreas Möller and Jürgen Klinsmann, who would turn 34 in a few weeks time and get stretchered off later in the tournament after being struck in the back by a free kick.

On the day of this big, fraught game things started slowly. I got to the Stade de Gerland at 10.30am. The entrance to the press centre in Lyon was decorated with a large stretch of astroturf with pink plastic tulips growing out of it. Surrounding this were a series of huge fish tanks etched with maps of the city. Fat, bug-eyed golden carp glided about inside. To get that far you had to present your pass and go through a metal detector. One day an Irish journalist asked the security guard if they ever had to confiscate anything illegal. The guard showed him a cardboard box which contained several switch blades, a Bowie knife and a set of brass knuckle dusters. 'Jeez,' he said to me. 'Some of these foreign press fellas don't fuck about.'

Kick-off wasn't until nine in the evening, but I had copy to file and, since I had a limited budget, I wanted to take full advantage of the free coffee and croissants. Ahead of me in the queue a senior BBC commentator whinged about the slowness of the service, while to my rear Ian St John smiled cheerfully and winked. At 11.30am a FIFA directive came around saying that places in the press stand were oversubscribed and a waiting list was being drawn up. Usually, the first pick of tickets went to journalists of the competing countries, but back in 1998 the mainstream US media took about as much interest in soccer as they did in the politics of Liechtenstein, while Iranian journalists were almost outnumbered by those from the Falkland Islands (a bloke from Port Stanley who supported Preston North End). When the confirmed list came around my name was on it.

The vast temporary hangar that housed the Lyon press centre filled up fast and early. By noon all 300 workstations were taken. From outside you could already hear the drumming that seemed to prefigure every game thudding through the walls. The PA system bleeped into life every 30 seconds with bureaucratic announcements about photographers' briefings and bib collection, the colour coding of those bibs, and the collection of lost camera equipment. Every one of them was made in four languages. A reporter sitting opposite me, who had a looming deadline, slammed his desk and said, 'Why do they send so many of the tossers anyway? They all take the same fucking picture.' Which was utterly untrue but entirely understandable.

Despite the fact that there were no-smoking signs up everywhere the air was quickly filled with tobacco haze. A reporter from *The Mirror* gestured across to a Colombian TV crew, 'Look, there's one of those fuckers smoking a pipe.'

FR Yugoslavia v Germany came on the TV screens. Journalists and photographers abandoned their laptops and grouped around the television with commentary in their native language. This didn't always work as planned. Sometimes the TV channels switched suddenly and inexplicably. One minute you'd be watching Scotland v Norway, the next an episode of the daytime US soap opera *The Bold and the Beautiful* dubbed into German.

There were no such problems that day. The game was decent – a 2-2 draw. The most memorable incident came when Dragan Stoijković scored his country's second, and Yugoslav coach Slobodan Santrać ran along the touchline in celebration of his team's goal only to suddenly pull up, grimacing in pain and clutching his hamstring. The laughter that followed rolled round and round the press centre from linguistic group to linguistic group. Journalists of the world united by schadenfreude and professional cynicism.

Perhaps there was a tinge of nervousness behind it too. Because a rumour was going around that 7,000 tickets for the game had been bought on the black market by members of the Iraq-sponsored Iranian dissident group the People's Mujahedin of Iran (MEK). Most football writers had no idea who MEK were, but those who knew how to use the Ask Jeeves web search engine on the media centre's mighty computers quickly discovered that MEK was led by a woman named Maryam Rajavi, had carried out violent attacks on Iranian embassies around the globe and were listed as a terrorist organisation by just about everybody in the western world.

I went up to the press stand an hour before kick-off. Huddles of Compagnies Républicaines de Sécurité (CRS) riot police clustered around the concourses, red packs of tear gas on their backs and their shields stacked. A police marksman perched behind my workstation, rifle on a tripod, cheeks marked with anti-glare make-up stripes, his telescopic sight trained on the opposite stand.

Already the noise was extraordinary. From the south stand, behind one goal, where a mass of Iranian supporters were gathered, came wave after wave of shrill chanting and whistling. When Ricky Martin's 'Macarena' came on the PA, as it did before every game, a young woman in a white mini skirt, crop top and white vinyl knee-high boots, her face painted in the colours of the Iranian flag, go-go danced on her chair waving a flag bearing an image of the MEK leader. Were these the dangerous terrorists we had been warned about? David Lacey, a man whose extreme reticence gave him a forbidding priestly air, turned and said, 'It reminds me of a women's hockey international at Wembley multiplied by a hundred.' The biggest danger seemed to be to our eardrums.

The teams came out to the usual plangent synthesiser music, thankfully barely audible above the din. The handshake has become an essential part of football's fractiousness. Managers harrumph that a proffered hand has been ignored, players pointedly refuse the outstretched mitt of an opponent who has wronged them. The handshakes before the USA Iran game were possibly the start of it all. According to FIFA protocol, Iran as 'Team B' in the match should advance towards the US ('Team A') for the handshake. However, it was soon revealed that the Supreme Leader of Iran, Ali Khamenei, had ordered the players not to do so. Behind the scenes FIFA negotiated with the

US team, who agreed to make the first move. The handshake went off cheerfully. The Iranian players presented their opponents with white roses as a sign of peace and the two teams posed together before kick-off, arms around each other's shoulders. It was the sort of image FIFA revelled in, proof of the healing power of the game, of the congeniality of what the organisation's bumptious president, Sepp Blatter, insisted on calling 'the football family'. The scenes in the stands, meanwhile, were the sort of thing that had Blatter sweating in his silk pyjamas.

As 9pm approached, huge anti-Khamenei banners and T-shirts decorated with pictures of Maryam Rajavi started to appear around the ground. Three minutes before kick-off a large orange balloon with a portrait of Rajavi suspended from it floated across the pitch, bobbed over the heads of the Iranian players and was eventually captured by referee Meier on the halfway line. I looked down at the TV monitor at my workstation to get a close-up of the image, but the screen was showing pictures of some pretty American girls in the crowd. The images on the monitor lagged a few seconds behind those on the pitch, so that you had a persistent sense of déjà vu, but this was different. The TV cameras were resolutely pointed away from the stand behind the goal where the bulk of the MEK protestors were located. They would stay that way. Television viewers around the world would have no idea what was going on.

When the game started, a mass of stewards appeared and began wading into the supporters in the south stand. Normally the stewards wore red Adidas tops, but this group had blue and black uniforms and orange armbands. 'Rozzers in disguise, got to be,' a bloke from *The Mirror* opined. It seemed a reasonable conclusion as the stewards battled to confiscate the dozens of 12ft by 5ft anti-Khamenei flags that had – according to a young American photojournalist who had been in among it – been smuggled into the stadium wrapped around bodies and then affixed to poles that had suddenly appeared from trouser legs. The battles went on for two hours. And through it all the chanting never let up. The noise level in the stadium varied from very, very loud to the absolutely extraordinarily loud. 'Fuck's sake,' the bloke from *The Express* said. 'Last time my head was ringing like this was after a Motörhead gig.'

Later that night the US photojournalist and I sat down for dinner in the cavernous but brilliant Brasserie Georges and he paraphrased an old ice-hockey joke, 'Tonight I was watching a political protest when all of a sudden a soccer game broke out.' Yet you can watch the match on YouTube and not get any sense of that. The protests are comprehensively airbrushed out, like a disgraced Politburo member from a Stalinist photo.

Even for those whose job it was, events on the field were hard to register in the frenzied atmosphere. Before the match, US midfielder Tab Ramos had speculated that the game meant less to the US players than it did to their opponents. While Khodadad Azizi had referenced the dead of the Iran-Iraq War before the game saying, 'Many families of martyrs are expecting us to win,' Ramos shrugged off the politics and said, 'You know, I don't hear anyone in training saying, "Let's go out there and win it for Bill Clinton."'

If the Iranians were more motivated than their opponents it didn't show in the opening moments. Only four minutes had gone when a free kick from Claudio Reyna reached McBride whose header cannoned off the bar with Ahmadreza Abedzadeh flailing. When Iran finally mounted a serious attack it was Azizi – who was wearing ridiculous mustard-coloured boots – who burst through one-on-one with Keller. The American keeper brought him down for a penalty so stonewall you could have carved your name on it. Urs Meier thought differently and waved play on.

The traditional frenzied discussion of which player's pass had precipitated the event was brought to a halt by a sudden bellowing laugh. Fingers pointed. There, amid the frenzy behind the goal, hoisted amid the fighting, was a union flag with the legend 'Fleetwood FC' on it.

Azizi's tumble was a brief moment of excitement for Iran. The USA continued to press, the excellent Reyna driving in a shot from 20 yards that struck a post. It was Iran who scored first, though, Javad Zarincheh's cross headed home by Hamid Estili. Azizi almost added a second a few minutes later but blasted an easy chance wide.

In the second period the US hit the woodwork for a third time and Abedzadeh saved acrobatically from Frankie Hejduk, a full-back with attacking tendencies and a face like an anteater. Flashbulbs were popping continually in the stand behind the goal now and files of CRS trotted along the touchline, shields and batons ready. Later FIFA would explain that, with their efforts at attracting the TV cameras thwarted, the MEK activists had planned a mass pitch invasion. The French authorities would not deploy the CRS unless the situation was serious and 'the situation was serious', a spokesman said defiantly. Well, perhaps, though as a friend of mine who was teaching at a lycée in Toulouse at the time remarked, 'The French will send in the riot police to quell a fight at the school gate.'

The game went on, the flashbulbs popped, whistles shrilled. When Iran's full-back Mehdi Mahdavikia pounced on a loose pass on the halfway line and ran 35 yards before whipping a shot past Keller and into the net the noise reached such a crazy pitch you feared the goldfish tanks in the media centre might explode. With a couple of minutes to go and the US attacking desperately, McBride – who had swatted the Iranian defence around all night like a competitive dad in a primary school kickabout – bundled the ball into the net after Abedzadeh fumbled.

It was the last action. Well, almost. As the final whistle went one of the Iranian fans behind the goal finally broke through the police and stewards and sprinted across the field waving his flag. A platoon of officers smacked him to the ground. The TV monitors showed only the celebrating Iranian players. The producers and camera crews had worked so diligently that MEK's strenuous efforts to attract the attention of a worldwide audience to their cause had comprehensively failed. They would have had more success putting anti-Khamenei leaflets in bottles and chucking them in the Rhône.

Back in the media centre, British journalists expressed disquiet at what the TV had chosen to show, or rather not to show. The complete blackout of what had been a peaceful political protest seemed like something from a totalitarian state rather than a modern Western democracy such as France.

But, of course, we were not actually in France. Entering the stadium, you crossed the border into FIFAland, a capitalist utopia with its own laws and customs, where politics and religion did not exist and the only true faith was profit. The ruling elite of FIFAland employed children to carry on the flags of countries with criminal human rights records, and proclaimed adherence to Corinthian ideals of sportsmanship but banned players from swapping shirts at the end of the game lest it offend the kit manufacturers. They introduced all kinds of rules to speed up the game but would not have ball boys or girls on the touchline because it would block the advertising hoardings. To complain that it was undemocratic was to miss the point.

The president of FIFAland, Sepp Blatter, had acted as swiftly against the MEK protestors as he would at a later tournament when a Dutch brewery threatened a guerrilla marketing campaign at matches. Whether you were protesting against a brutal and repressive political regime or promoting non-official lager, you had no place in FIFAland.

Even if you accepted this reality, it was hard not to revel in the irony. At the end of USA v Iran, as the CRS gathered across the front of the south stand, tear-gas canisters at the ready, and a group of the special stewards gradually pressed the protestors back through the exits using shields and truncheons, a jovial announcer came on the PA, as he did after every game, thanked us all for coming and making the game such a special occasion and reminded us that this was FIFA 'fair play day'.

After the announcement had finished, the man from *The Telegraph* turned to me with a bitter smile, 'It's like Hunter S. Thompson said, "Who needs drugs when reality's this twisted?"'

Statuesque
by Samindra Kunti

Feyenoord v Borussia Dortmund
UEFA Cup Final
Rotterdam, the Netherlands
8 May 2002

In the wake of George Floyd's death, Europeans toppled historical statues of slave owners to confront the past. In Britain, protestors tore down the bronze statue of Edward Colston, a 17th-century slave trader. Across the Channel, the statue of Belgian King Leopold II, who exploited and brutalised Congo, was targeted and then removed by local authorities. In France, Jean-Baptiste Colbert's statue was vandalised. In the 17th century, he had helped write the *Code Noir*, defining the conditions of slavery in the French colonial empire.

The wave of iconoclasm prompted a debate, between those who wanted to confront the West's often savage colonisation of Africa and others who argued that the past should be remembered and explained rather than obliterated.

In downtown Rotterdam, one statue survived. Pim Fortuyn's bust memorialises a tempestuous moment in Dutch contemporary political history and reflects how an idiosyncratic man rose to become a prominent national politician. His political ideas resonated with a wide audience. Fortuyn was not a slave trader, but he connected with Rotterdammers through speech that was often controversial, populist and xenophobic, feeding on festering resentment and hopelessness among the local working class.

In June, his statue was daubed with the word 'racist'. It shocked Rotterdammers, whose sentiments towards, and memories of, Fortuyn remain powerful. They still admire him. Members of FIIR, a group of young Feyenoord hooligans, rushed to the Korte Hoogstraat in the city centre to protect the statue from what they perceived to be vandalism. They unfurled a banner. It read 'Rotterdam, stand your ground'.

* * *

In 1970, Brazil defeated Italy 4-1 in the World Cup Final, a match that still represents a historic apex in the global game. That same year Feyenoord's 2-1 win in the European Cup Final against Celtic heralded the advent of a sophisticated system of football and the glorious intricacies of the Dutch game. *Totaalvoetbal*, Johan Cruyff, 4-3-3, possession and passing swept the game and steered it towards more holistic philosophies. Following cultural liberalisation in the Netherlands, the Dutch reframed the game and its essence: football was about exploiting space. In *Brilliant Orange*, David Winner identifies spatial creativity, architecture and planning as cornerstones of the Dutch conceptualisation of the game.

Feyenoord's football was less intellectual, even if a reader of the Scottish magazine *Celtic View* poignantly wrote after the match, 'Feyenoord's maddening, clinical, almost military, precision of successive forward, diagonal, backward and triangular traceries was more in keeping with a geometrical exercise than a cup final. Irritating to watch to a degree – but it got them the European Cup.'

The triangulations both shocked and confused the reader, but his words are instructive: Dutch football was cultured and complicated to understand. It represented a formation and ideas that were historically more complex. Feyenoord's game was about more than simply grit. Ernst Happel's team married mettle with métier. They played an elegant and balanced 4-3-3 formation in which captain Rinus Israël anchored a very solid back line. Midfield metronome Willem van Hanegem wedded superb tackling with gossamer passing skills. He played alongside Franz Hasil, a product of the Austrian school. In attack, Ove Kindvall was the focal point. The Swedish striker was a classic and intelligent number nine who scored a prolific 129 goals in 144 matches between 1966 and 1971 at Feyenoord.

In extra time of the European Cup Final, three minutes from the end, Kindvall made sure Feyenoord were crowned continental champions when Celtic's Billy McNeill misread a long ball and the Swede exploited the lax defending to secure a deserved 2-1 win. Feyenoord were the first Dutch club to top Europe, but even so, Ajax Amsterdam and the Dutch national team have always been credited for the rise of *totaalvoetbal*.

Historically, Amsterdam and Rotterdam have endured an antagonistic relationship. The capital and its club were symbiotic, reflecting one another – urbane, distinguished, extravagant, and, above all, home to the balletic Cruyff, the mercurial number 14 and disciple of Rinus Michels, the godfather of *totaalvoetbal*.

By the banks of the River Maas, there was little time for extravagance or artistry. In Rotterdam, the working masses laboured in Europe's biggest port. A local institution since 1908, Feyenoord appropriated that blue-collar ethos. The connection between the club and its fans was deeply intuitive. In 1940, the Germans had flattened the city centre during the Rotterdam Blitz, but they played through the Second World War. Feyenoord rejected the virtues Ajax propagated, adopting the traditional tenets of the city – vigour, sweat and hard work. The club and its supporters were too confident to ever feel diminished by the Ajax bourgeoisie.

But the towering legacy of Happel's luminous, compelling team and their victory in 1970 weighed Feyenoord down. The triumph had somehow been transgressive. In the years to come, Feyenoord exhibited other, more mundane qualities with escalating confidence. They were never to recapture that 1970s magic and the innocence a virgin trophy engenders. That victory became a strangely haunting image for a club that always finds ways to wander and self-destruct. At Feyenoord, every triumph is the portent of a tragedy.

It was no different in 1999 when the Rotterdam team won the Dutch league under coach Leo Beenhakker. In the afterglow of the title, the club wanted to ensure a bright future, but invested poorly. Although they did make one wise decision. Bert van Marwijk, then a young coach, arrived in Rotterdam a year later.

Van Marwijk had built his credentials at Fortuna Sittard, reaching the Dutch Cup Final with the modest club, but his move to Rotterdam propelled him into the limelight at one of the Netherlands' biggest sporting institutions, where both the board and fans were unforgiving. The 1999 title, six years after their previous domestic crown, had engaged the volatile 'Legioen', the nickname of Feyenoord's fanbase, evoking a sudden moment of fantasy in which Feyenoord could compete with Ajax and PSV Eindhoven.

The young coach's own memories of Feyenoord also kindled strong emotions. During his playing days, Van Marwijk had three chances to play for Feyenoord. As a teenager, he had featured in the final of the Feyenoord Toernooi, a renowned international youth tournament. 'I was 14, 15 and you played the warm-up game [the final] in De Kuip in front of 25,000 fans,' remembers Van Marwijk. 'That was unforgettable. Feyenoord was simply a very, very big club, and it still is. That moved me.'

In Van Marwijk's first season, Feyenoord finished as runners-up behind PSV. They had led the table comfortably but collapsed after the winter break. The following season the same scenario materialised. On the face of it, Feyenoord simply ran out of steam in the second half of the campaign, but discontent stirred.

Players rejected Van Marwijk's coaching philosophy. At times, captain Paul Bosvelt and defender Kees van Wonderen, two veterans, clashed with the coach, but there was enough discernment and emotional intelligence to tolerate differing views in the dressing room. 'It was an articulate team, who would tell each other the hard truth,' says Van Marwijk.

Striker Pierre van Hooijdonk understood that they were a tough collection of personalities to manage. 'It wasn't the easiest of groups for a young coach,' he says. 'The team was relatively experienced, with a few seasoned players. Bert wanted to control everything. It got edgy after the winter break, but, as a coach and person, Bert wasn't an asshole. There was mutual respect.'

Van Hooijdonk had arrived at Feyenoord in his early 30s having made waves in Scotland and England (for different reasons). He signed from Benfica where the lanky striker became surplus to requirements when a new club chairman seized control, even though he had cost the club 14m guilder (around €6.4m euros at the time), scored 22 goals in 30 matches and reclaimed his spot with Oranje.

In the autumn, the Rotterdam club had been a bit of a misfit in the Champions League. Even in 2001, well before Roman Abramovich kick-started the age of the super clubs with his acquisition of Chelsea, Dutch clubs simply couldn't compete with the continental elite. In Group H, they finished third behind Bayern Munich and Sparta Prague. With the window of opportunity quickly fading in the Dutch league, Feyenoord and Van Hooijdonk were left with the UEFA Cup to save the season. There was an added motivation, too: the 2002 final would be held in Rotterdam.

Van Hooijdonk believes that Feyenoord had no business in the UEFA Cup, let alone the Champions League. Van Marwijk sees it somewhat differently: Feyenoord never assembled the best players, but his team gelled. They were a strong unit. Dutch veterans formed the spine of the team with an eclectic group of foreign talents providing not only technique but also zeal and zest.

Van Wonderen and Patrick Paauwe anchored the back line. As former midfielders, they were assets in Feyenoord's build-up play. In midfield, the captain was the engine, whose water-carrying attitude embodied the quintessential Feyenoord player. Up front, Van Hooijdonk had to deliver goals.

Van Marwijk also singles out both Shinji Ono and Jon Dahl Tomasson for praise. 'Ono played alongside Bosvelt,' he says. 'He was a very good Japanese player, who acclimated very quickly and became a fan favourite.

Very creative and very skilful. He also chipped in defensively. Paul and him were two number sixes, but Ono was also the connection with the attack. They could both score a goal. Tomasson was a shuttling player at number ten. Jon Dahl was so important for the team – he ensured that we pressed. Bosvelt and Ono dared to defend higher than their opponent, which meant that your back line moved higher. We would press with our 4-4-2 system, but in possession Tomasson would often play higher than Van Hooijdonk. When we got dispossessed, he tracked back lightning-quick.'

It was a formidable team, but still one that all together cost less than Zlatan Ibrahimović. Feyenoord's UEFA Cup run wasn't shorn of irony either. They still encountered clubs that were out of their league and teams whose qualities outstripped anything Van Marwijk's 11 could supposedly muster. In the fourth round, Feyenoord eliminated Glasgow Rangers 4-3 on aggregate. But it was in the quarter-finals against PSV that Feyenoord's UEFA Cup campaign truly ignited in the hearts and minds of the club and Het Legioen. Van Hooijdonk's dramatic late header in the second leg kept Feyenoord in the tie before Van Marwijk's team prevailed from the penalty spot. 'It was a very explosive tie,' says reporter and Feyenoord fan Joost de Jong. 'PSV's Mark van Bommel was Van Marwijk's son-in-law. That gripped us. Something happened at De Kuip. It was almost an electric shock. You knew that we would never roar like that again.'

After PSV, the final at home in De Kuip became something tangible. 'That was when the belief came,' recalls Van Hooijdonk. They first had to navigate a semi-final against Inter Milan, a team sprinkled in stardust thanks to the likes of Ronaldo, Christian Vieri and Clarence Seedorf. The San Siro had also been the venue of Feyenoord's 1970 conquest and 10,000 Dutch fans traveled to Milan for a 1-0 victory after Ivan Cordoba's own goal en route to a 3-2 aggregate win and a ticket for the final.

'We won 1-0 against a very good, but arrogant team,' explains Van Marwijk. 'I noticed that during the warm-up. Our team was well built and everyone knew his duties. We weren't easily impressed. At home, we had to defend the advantage. It turned into a nerve-racking game, 2-2! In the very last seconds, Ronaldo got a chance, but, even before the game, the match captivated us. I heard our boys say, "We are not going to let this be taken from us."'

With seven goals, van Hooijdonk had been instrumental on the way to the final. Pundits and commentators branded the competition the 'Pierre van Hooijdonk Cup', the hyperbole a testimony to how smitten everyone had become with him. At first they had been reluctant to accept Van Hooijdonk. The centre-forward with Moroccan roots swayed the sceptical fanbase with his two free kicks against Rangers and decisive headers against both PSV and Inter. His goals and glories at the club never came wrapped in a diva's narcissism but with a down-to-earth attitude, something that would make a Nottingham Forest supporter choke on their beer. He shepherded his club to the grand final. Van Hooijdonk, Feyenoord and Rotterdam were primed for the game of their lives.

* * *

It was the Netherlands' 9/11: everyone remembers it and everyone remembers what they were doing the moment that trivial Monday afternoon in May 2002 turned dark. Van Marwijk remembers it, Van Hooijdonk remembers it and so do de Jong and Ivo Opstelten, the then mayor and member of the conservative-liberal party Volkspartij voor Vrijheid en Democratie (VVD, the People's Party for Freedom and Democracy). The coach was at a hotel, the striker on the way home from training, the mayor in a meeting and reporter de Jong researching a story. With shock, they learned the news: politician Pim Fortuyn had been assassinated.

That morning, Fortuyn had visited De Kuip, the venue for the UEFA Cup Final between Feyenoord and Borussia Dortmund taking place two days later. Fortuyn wasn't exactly the biggest fan of football. In 1996 he had navigated his way home among drunk Dutch and German supporters ahead of a friendly game. The intoxicated Germans had clashed with local police and some of them even performed Nazi salutes. Immaculately dressed and with a briefcase in hand, Fortuyn frowned at all the adults, their orange paraphernalia and the mounted police chasing visiting fans. Why all the fuss about a simple leather ball?

At last, he returned to the street where he lived. For many years the Randweg was a safe space, a comfort zone as well as a strategic base camp overlooking Hillesluis, one of Rotterdam's poorest neighbourhoods that lies adjacent to De Kuip. Fortuyn was an anomaly in the Randweg. He taught sociology at the university and his preference for cigars, wines, suits and expensive cars was extravagant. The local kids fawned over his Bentley. He had no connection with Hillesluis, where poverty, unemployment and petty crime reigned. There was no future in Hillesluis even less so for immigrants.

But it allowed Fortuyn to observe the rich and sometimes raw tapestry of the local underclass, those workers who had been forgotten in an ever-more globalised world. In the end, what had all their labour yielded, apart from misery in a destitute area on the south bank of the Maas? Fortuyn articulated what workers in Hillesluis and other deprived areas of the city had felt, but with a bravura and braggadocio that was almost un-Dutch. He criticised the political establishment and offered outspoken opinions on popular themes like integration and crime. He called Islam 'retarded'.

Quickly, Fortuyn's opponents branded him a right-wing agitator in the vein of Flanders's Filip Dewinter and France's Jean-Marie Le Pen. Europe's far-right found a common scapegoat in economic migrants, refugees and especially Islam.

'They *said* he was a populist,' counters Opstelten. 'He was an intellectual. He wrote a lot. His weekly column in *Elsevier* was well read and he identified a number of things with which a lot of people agreed. For example, the issue of safety in the city and the country. The issue that in many neighbourhoods the population was changing and as a result entire neighbourhoods were changing, in which the people no longer recognised themselves.'

Van Marwijk didn't vote for Fortuyn, but also didn't see in him a far-right politician even though a sizeable number in the Netherlands – quite legitimately, given his outspoken Islamophobia – thought that he was. Still, Van Hooijdonk echoes his coach's ideas, dismissing the portrayal of Fortuyn as a populist politician. 'Fortuyn was so popular that he was at the point of becoming prime minister,' says Van Hooijdonk. 'He had very clear ideas. If I compare him to [far-right politician Geert] Wilders, he was a bit more tactful.'

De Jong voted for Fortuyn. 'There were problems with minorities, immigrants and foreigners, namely Moroccans,' he says. 'Fortuyn labelled this in an open and hard way, but without being villainous. He represented hope to many people. That things would change, in the old neighbourhoods. He had something about him, but he was also extreme.'

'It was a kind of wake-up call for the existing politics, because all parties lost one way or another,' says Opstelten. 'A new style of political discourse emerged and that also led to a reset in policy priorities. He was polarising towards other parties.'

Fortuyn's rise seemed unstoppable. He resonated with Rotterdammers despite his open homosexuality and butler at his new home, the Palazzo di Pietro. Born in northern Holland, Fortuyn was nurturing his dream of transforming and modernising the Netherlands. He was a baby boomer, enlightened but struggling with the existing political order.

On the day he died, visiting De Kuip, he acquiesced to pose with a Feyenoord cap. Of course, he wasn't a Feyenoord supporter, but it would have been crass to refuse this small request. Fortuyn understood Rotterdammers and Rotterdammers understood him. A poll confirmed Fortuyn's huge popularity. He was perhaps on course for the highest political office in the country. In March, Leefbaar Rotterdam (Liveable Rotterdam) captured 17 seats in the local council elections. It was a surprising and sweeping win after Fortuyn had been expelled from Leefbaar Nederland, the national party. The Labour party, the PvdA, was left bleeding, but Rotterdam is often a bellwether for sentiments in other parts of the country.

Fortuyn was rising and rising. Then, at 6.05pm that Monday, in the car park of Hilversum's Media Park, Volkert van der Graaf, an environmental and animal-rights activist, emerged from a thicket and shot Fortuyn multiple times from close range.

In his office, Opstelten first verified the news before switching on the TV with city council members and aldermen. Information was fragmented, but by the time Fortuyn passed away, the magnitude of his death could not be overstated. It was the first political murder in the contemporary history of the Netherlands. 'That's the biggest shock you can get in a democracy when a directly elected representative is shot dead,' laments Opstelten.

As the political establishment and the media contemplated Fortuyn's death, emotions stirred across Rotterdam and across the Netherlands. In The Hague, the *Binnenhof*, the prime minister's office, required police protection. Hillesluis emptied. Some walked to the city centre to vent their emotions, others later queued at the condolence register Opstelten had organised at town hall. Rotterdammers, Feyenoord fans, immigrants and people from all walks of life clamoured to bid Fortuyn farewell. A large banner read, 'Pim, you were murdered. But your ideas weren't.' Nearby, a column graced Voltaire's words, 'I disapprove of what you say, but I will defend to the death your right to say it.'

* * *

Suddenly, the UEFA Cup Final felt irrelevant. It was tragic for Feyenoord as well: they had briefly escaped Ajax's shadow, but Pim Fortuyn's murder relegated the final to a background story. As a mix of consternation, anger, anxiety and sadness descended over Rotterdam, the mayor, the police and the public prosecutor convened and determined without pressure from UEFA – according to Opstelten – that the final would go ahead. 'The match had to be played because that was in the spirit of Fortuyn as well,' explains Opstelten. 'Life goes on despite the terrible situation. That's what the match signalled. I never doubted the decision.'

Opstelten asked UEFA for a minute of silence before kick-off, black armbands and zero tolerance for inciting chants in the stands. He also outlawed any festivities at the Coolsingel, the beating heart of Rotterdam's city centre and backdrop to all of Feyenoord's historic victory parades. Opstelten acted with an efficiency that was perhaps difficult to achieve at Feyenoord with its myriad of characters and additional pressure ahead of a major final.

At the pre-match news conference, journalists bombarded both Van Marwijk and Van Hooijdonk with questions about Fortuyn, much to the dismay of UEFA's media officer. It was an unprecedented situation and Van Marwijk said as much at the time: 'I am not sure what to do with it.'

Van Marwijk recalls today, 'We also spoke to the team about it; how did they view it?'. In the end, the general consensus was that Fortuyn would have wanted us to play. That filtered through to the club and the team.'

Van Hooijdonk and the players were obsessed with the cup, even if Fortuyn's murder was a reminder that football was a sideshow in life. They trained and prepared with the zeal and focus that professionalism and a European cup final required from the players. 'It is very easy to reply in a politically correct manner, but as a player you live in a selfish cocoon,' admits Van Hooijdonk. 'You think there is nothing more important than the final.'

Back in Rotterdam, de Jong didn't care much any more for what was to be his first European club final as a Feyenoord fan and a thrilling end to the season. On match days, he often shared a beer with his brother-in-law and chatted excitedly about the game. This time, it all felt perfunctory, strangely inappropriate. De Jong and Feyenoord fans no longer yearned for European glory. Instead, they talked endlessly about Fortuyn, processing his murder and the grief that came with it. 'It remains bizarre that the match went ahead,' feels de Jong. 'Football is important, but it isn't.'

Once at De Kuip, some sense of relief and reassurance set in. This was home and the importance of a UEFA Cup Final couldn't entirely be discounted. 'There was a very strange atmosphere before the game,' remembers Van Marwijk. 'You noticed and felt it during the warm-up, but when the referee blew for the kick-off the timidity vanished and it turned into a real final.'

A few days earlier, Van Marwijk had watched Dortmund clinch the German Bundesliga title against Werder Bremen. Matthias Sammer's side were formidable with a mix of German stalwarts and Brazilian talents, but what struck Van Marwijk most was Dortmund's 'organised chaos', as he describes it. 'It was a very difficult team to analyse because they actually really moved all over the field, except for the goalkeeper, the central defenders and [Stefan] Reuter, a holding midfielder,' he says. 'They all stuck to their positions. The rest just moved! It was very important to play such a team without the temptation of getting dragged out of position. You have to learn to defend the spaces, except not like 30 years ago when zonal marking arrived, without any pressure on the ball. We defended the spaces but pressured the ball whenever possible.'

Feyenoord took the lead after Jürgen Kohler gave away a penalty and was sent off in the final game of his distinguished career. Van Hooijdonk stepped forward for what many consider the defining few minutes of his career. He scored the penalty. Minutes earlier, Feyenoord's number nine had struck the woodwork from a set piece. Van Marwijk knew what was about to happen when Van Hooijdonk got a second chance. 'I said to Mario Been and John Metgod, my assistants, "This one is going to go in because [goalkeeper Jens] Lehmann was positioned in the same spot, a little past the centre of the goal,"' he says. 'I knew immediately this was going to be a goal. If he took three free kicks and missed the first two, there was almost a guarantee that the third one would go in.'

Van Hooijdonk considers the conversion rate the true hallmark of a free-kick specialist. 'Cristiano Ronaldo just scored a free kick at Juventus and that was his first free-kick goal in 42 free kicks,' says Van Hooijdonk. 'It is not the number that matters, but the ratio to the number of games and the number of attempts. Ronaldo is still labelled as a free-kick specialist, and yet he is not alone.'

In De Kuip, van Hooijdonk stood at 90 degrees next to the ball, rather than behind it. He took a few loping, almost gazelle-like strides before he struck the ball with his instep. With impeccable accuracy, the ball whizzed past Jens Lehmann. Van Hooijdonk, lifting his shirt, wheeled away in celebration. The fans bellowed, 'Puje-ens-ufopierre! Puje-ens-ufopierre!'

Badly positioned, the German keeper had been too late to prevent the goal. He should have known better. Speed always accompanied Van Hooijdonk's accuracy. It's what set him apart from other set-piece specialists. Van Marwijk describes his free kicks as a mix of Dutch players Willem van Hanegem and Kees Kist, and computer scientist Kristen Nygaard because he combined power, refinement and curve. 'Van Hooijdonk united all three,' says Van Marwijk. 'Pierre was an autodidact.'

Still, 2-0 up, facing opponents that were down to ten men, Feyenoord should have been home and dry. Instead Feyenoord were overwhelmed for much of the second half. Dortmund's game gravitated towards their young Czech midfielder Tomáš Rosický with Dedé providing attacking impetus from the wing, Jan Koller dropping deep from his number nine position and Lars Ricken drifting inside. A Márcio Amoroso penalty cut the deficit, before Jon Dahl Tomasson restored Feyenoord's two-goal lead. But, even though they were trailing 3-1, Dortmund were quicker and more alert than their hosts. Koller scored to make it 3-2. Dortmund went on the attack. But Feyenoord held on for a famous victory.

Van Hooijdonk had transcended himself that night. I had been in the crowd with my mum who would drive me all across Europe to watch games. It was my first European final. I was 14, too young to understand the significance of the match or Fortuyn's assassination. Nor could I make out the chanting after Van Hooijdonk's free kick. It was only on the way home, in the car, with my mum at the wheel of our vintage Audi 100, and with the radio on, that I understood the song the local fans had belted out all night long, 'Puje – ens – ufopierre!' Or, in English, 'Put your hands up for Pierre!'

Feyenoord had a new hero, and the city and the country a martyr they would never forget.

Heavy Metal Futebol
by Andrew Downie

Corinthians v River Plate
Copa Libertadores
São Paulo, Brazil
4 May 2006

I need to make something clear right from the start. I live in Brazil so all games are away games to me. Home is Easter Road and always will be. Everything else is away, whether that's Pittodrie, Old Trafford or the Maracanã. Home is where the heart is. I know that sounds a bit twee, but it's true.

Brazilians often ask me, 'What's your team in Brazil?' I always say Hibs. Hibs are my team no matter what country I'm in. Sometimes they laugh. More often I get a puzzled look and they think I misunderstood. No, they repeat, 'What Brazilian team do you support?'

Well, the truth is there isn't one. In Brazil you can either *torcer* for a team, which is to support them, or you can *simpatizar* with one, which is to have a soft spot for them. So sometimes I say I have a soft spot for Botafogo, because I used to live in Rio and I translated the biography of Garrincha. And sometimes I say I have a soft spot for Santos, which is true, because they had Pelé and Robinho and Neymar and always try to play attractive football. When I'm in São Paulo and I'm talking with *Corinthianos* – that's what they call Corinthians fans – I sometimes say that I have a soft spot for them because of Sócrates and because they have the best fans in the country, which is also kind of true.

So I support Hibs. Everywhere.

But Easter Road is a long way away and the Pacaembu stadium is just down the road from my house. I wouldn't say I chose to live in the Higienópolis neighbourhood because the Pacaembu was close, but it was definitely a big plus. The Pacaembu is essentially at the end of my street, a ten-minute walk away, down a very steep hill. I come out my door and walk along Rua Alagoas past the Parque Buenos Aires on the right, sometimes stopping in the Barcelona bakery for a pastry, and down past the FAAP university building, all neo-classical columns and neo-riche students.

Where the road ends, just over to the left, you can see the magnificent art-deco facade of the Pacaembu.

Its proper name is Estádio Municipal Paulo Machado de Carvalho, named after the man who led the Brazilian delegations to victory at the 1958 and 1962 World Cups. Above the big gates to the stadium, at the far side of the Praça Charles Miller, a vast open space named after the son of a Scottish father and Brazilian mother who brought football to Brazil in 1894, that whole title is spelt out in beautiful art-deco lettering.

On the days and nights of big games, my street fills up with parked cars and fans making their way to the ground, in ones and twos, their shirts on and their flags in hand. Sometimes whole columns of fans march by, chanting and letting off firecrackers that bang and crackle right outside my window. If the wind is blowing in the right direction and the traffic isn't too heavy which, to be honest, is almost never because the traffic is always heavy in São Paulo, you can hear the roar of the crowd outside my window. Or maybe that's wishful thinking because I love hearing the roar of the crowd. There's nothing like hearing that eruption of noise when you're outside a stadium. Unless it comes from the away end, then it's the most horrible thing in the world.

The reason I'm telling you all this is that one of the most unforgettable games I ever saw was at the Pacaembu. It was a Copa Libertadores game in May 2006. Corinthians were at home to River Plate in the second leg of a last-16 tie. It wasn't that common for Corinthians to qualify for the Libertadores back then. The thing about Corinthians is they are a massive club but their fans didn't always get the trophies their support deserved. It's hard to think of a similar club outside Brazil. Perhaps Newcastle in England? Schalke in Germany? Hammarby in Sweden? By that I mean they have a huge number of fans and loads of supporters in the media but there's always this sense of unfulfilled potential. Corinthians are more successful now, but back in 2006, them qualifying for the Libertadores was kind of unusual. They had only managed it six times in the previous 30 years. And they only made it as far as the semi-finals once. Disappointment and frustration were common.

The Corinthians fans were obsessed with winning the Libertadores. All their main rivals in São Paulo had won it at least once and some of them fairly recently. Palmeiras won it in 1999. São Paulo, who were the most successful team at the time, won it back-to-back in 1992 and 1993 and again just the year before in 2005. Santos hadn't won it for ages but they were Santos, one of the greatest club sides in history, so that didn't matter too much. Corinthians, though, had never won the Libertadores and it really rankled. It was like a sore that they couldn't stop picking. It festered and every year it would come back redder and rawer. Their rivals loved to wind them up about it.

Back then Corinthians were also the only one of São Paulo's big four not to own their own ground. They played their home games at the Pacaembu, which was owned by the city, or they hired the Morumbi, which they hated doing because it meant they were paying money to the owners, who were São Paulo. São Paulo already thought they were the elite club and Corinthians were riff-raff. All these things together contributed to Corinthians feeling like they were the poor relations in the city.

You're probably wondering why I'm going on about all this rather than the actual football. Well, the best answer is that going to an away game is not really about the football, is it? Or it's only partly about the football. Really, it's about the day out. The ride there, the drink in a new pub beforehand, different pies at half-time. These are the things that you look forward to. That's what sticks in the mind. And that's doubly the case when you're abroad. Because when you're in a foreign country everything is already novel. And so it's already more of an adventure. And it never gets old for me, that going to a new ground, seeing the bars around about, hanging with the fans beforehand, seeing what they look like, hearing their songs, just soaking in the atmosphere. It's brilliant.

I'll get to the football in a second, but all this talk of novelties at the football reminds me of something. I once took an American editor of mine to see Portuguesa play in São Paulo. Portuguesa were the fifth-biggest team in the city and the only one at home the Sunday he was visiting from New York. The thing he most remembers was the old bloke who walked round the ground selling peanuts. We paid about the equivalent of £1 and he poured a big pile of them on the concrete terrace beside us. We spent the whole of the first half sitting in the sun shelling nuts. I have absolutely no recollection of much else that day. Not the other team, not the score (although I can remember it was the same day that David Wotherspoon scored a 25-yard screamer for Hibs to knock Hearts out of the Scottish Cup). But I have stupidly fond memories of sitting there eating that big pile of nuts.

If I'm being honest I love everything about going to games in Brazil. Maybe even more than going to see Hibs. Because first and foremost there's no pressure. I've not got a dog in the fight, as they say. So I don't get stressed or wound up. I don't know the players as well, and it's harder to get annoyed at the ref. The result doesn't really matter to me. There are other reasons, too. If it's an afternoon match it's usually warm and I love lying back in the sun watching two teams I don't really care about, all for the pleasure of just watching a match. Even better if I am with a mate, we can just catch up with each other's lives while the football happens to be going on. The football is like the background music on a long car journey.

If it's a night match, then there's a whole new dimension to it. It's always more tense at night. Brazil is often tense after dark. Except in the tourist parts no one walks about at night because it's not safe. The streets are deserted. But on game nights there are always loads of supporters hanging about outside Pacaembu or the Morumbi. It can be scary. And it's a lot worse at say Vasco da Gama, whose beautiful old ground in Rio is surrounded by some rough neighbourhoods. One night I went there in a mate's car and when we came out the car was gone. I don't think I ever went back to Vasco.

It's also true that all these new sensations are sharper at night. The grass looks greener under the floodlights. The crowd noise is louder. The atmosphere is different. There's an immediacy to night games that isn't there on a sunny afternoon. The areas around the grounds in Brazil are usually packed with fans hanging out. For miles around the ground there are people on street corners shouting at cars and trying to wave them into their makeshift car parks. Entrepreneurs set up charcoal grills selling hamburgers and skewers of meat before and after the match. On every corner there's someone selling beer from polystyrene coolers filled with ice. The streets around Brazilian grounds are always alive at night and the closer it gets to kick-off the more tense things get.

It was like this the night Corinthians played River Plate. It was a weekday night. Corinthians were favourites, which was unusual given their record but it was merited this time around because they had won four of their six games in the group stages and had the third-best record of all 16 teams that made it to the knockout round. River Plate were only in the competition after squeaking through the qualifying stages and they had won three and lost three of their group games.

Brazil versus Argentina games always have a wee bit of extra needle to them but this one was especially tasty because of the recent history. A foreign-owned company called Media Sports Investment had ploughed big money into Corinthians and bought several players they couldn't normally afford. One of the key figures behind MSI was Kia Joorabchian who, three months later, would take Carlos Tevez and Javier Mascherano to West Ham.

The transfer of two big-name Argentines to Corinthians, Tevez from Boca and Mascherano from River Plate, for tens of millions of dollars, was unprecedented. Tevez hated River and usually went out of his way to wind them up. And then there was the Passarella factor. Daniel Passarella had been hired by Kia to be Corinthians manager the year before but he only lasted 15 games, which, to be honest, wasn't unusual for Brazil, where managers regularly get hired and fired after just a few weeks. Passarella was fired in May 2005 but Corinthians hadn't paid him his full whack when he left. He went back to Argentina, got a job in charge of River, and sued Corinthians for the money he was owed. Players suing former clubs to get what they were owed is about the most common thing in South American football. One ex-Santos player told me he once wrote off one million reais – the currency in Brazil – that the club owed him after he left. It was too much hassle to fight them through the courts. It never made the news. He founded his own church instead. I kid you not. Only in Brazil.

But Passarella was one man you do not want to cross. He never gave an inch, on or off the field. You could see how much he wanted to stick it to Corinthians. And there was also this superstitious Argentine thing going on. River had won the Libertadores twice before in 1986 and 1996 and this was 2006 so they were quite hopeful they would do it again and keep up that run. They had got to the final in 1966 and 1976 as well. Superstition is a big thing in Latin American football. After Brazil won the World Cup in Sweden in 1958 they got the same plane and the same pilot to fly them to Chile in 1962. The head of the delegation wore the same suit. The keeper wore the same old T-shirt under his jersey.

So you had the Argentine players at Corinthians, Passarella out for revenge, Corinthians desperate to win the Libertadores for the first time *and* the whole Argentina v Brazil nationalistic thing. It all added to the needle. You could feel the tension around the ground. I recall getting there early that night because I knew it might get interesting. I was already inside when hordes of Corinthians fans without tickets tried to force their way through the main gate and had to be pushed back by police. The Brazilian police didn't (and still don't) do softly softly. They wade in first chance they got.

Brazilian police can be brutal, although it's worse in Rio. I was out on patrol with the São Paulo police one night reporting a story I was doing for *Time* magazine and they stopped a bunch of youths on the edge of the city, where the poor parts are. The police were putting on a show for me, pretending to be respectful, but the lads were still forced against the wall, hands on their heads, feet apart, empty your pockets, all that. And one of them accidentally stood on a policeman's boot. He realised what he'd done and almost crapped himself. He got down on his knees and used the cuff of his shirt to rub the dust off the copper's shoe. He was petrified. If a reporter hadn't been there who knows what the police would have done.

Although the brutal reputation of the police meant nothing when a match was considered important enough. When a mate came to visit me from Edinburgh we went to see Botafogo v Fluminense at the Maracanã. For some reason the organisers had decided only to open part of the ground. I would usually just turn up at the Maracanã and buy tickets at the windows or pay an extra couple of quid and get one off a tout outside. There were always loads of touts. But because they had only opened part of the stadium, loads of fans were looking for tickets and none were on sale. My mate didn't speak Portuguese so I told him to wait while I took a walk round the ground and tried to find a tout. Except, for about the only time in my life, I couldn't find one. When I eventually made it back empty-handed, my mate was grinning at me and holding two tickets. Someone had come up to him and sold him a spare pair.

We were happy but most of the fans weren't. They were getting angry because they couldn't buy tickets to get inside a half-empty stadium. We made our way to the turnstiles and just as we got there a massive group of fans charged the entrance and started tearing at the big metal gates until the chains broke and the mob rushed forward. I grabbed my mate, shouted 'Run!' and charged in through the open gates in the middle of the crowd. We ran as fast as we could, up a couple of big concrete ramps, and on to the terraces inside. My mate couldn't understand why I insisted on joining the invading mob when we already had tickets. We'll remember this day forever, I told him. It was the day we invaded the Maracanã.

Back at the Pacaembu, some Corinthians fans tried to push their way into the ground early on and there was a real weird feeling in the air. You know when you just get this feeling that everything could kick off at any moment? The stadium was full ages before kick-off and there were still loads of people hanging around outside. The Pacaembu is not that big. The capacity back then was less than 40,000. A wee bit of the main stand was fenced off for River fans, leaving Corinthians with about 30,000 tickets. Corinthians could have sold twice as many.

The game itself was edgy right from the kick-off. Corinthians had lost the first leg 3-2 at the Monumental a week before but they were a bit unlucky. They had Mascherano sent off early on and Tevez, who had put them ahead early in the game, had a goal disallowed. He wasn't quite the Tevez we all know and love now but he definitely had all that manic energy about him. He was like a coked-up puppy chasing a boomerang and the Corinthians fans idolised him for it. They were confident they would overturn the deficit at home.

They started well. Remember a player called Nilmar? He was this quite slight centre-forward. Nippy and skilful but a bit lightweight, he had brief but successful spells at Olympique Lyon and Villarreal. He played for Brazil, too. Well, Nilmar put Corinthians 1-0 ahead a few minutes before half-time. If it stayed like that they were going through on away goals.

The place was rocking, which was just as well. It was May in São Paulo, which is winter, so it was freezing. It wasn't that balmy, shirtsleeves kind of weather people always think about when they think about Brazil. São Paulo can get cold in the winter. They call it the city of drizzle, because it has this really fine rain called *garoa*.

It's more of a cross between drizzle and fog really. And when it's cold and the *garoa* swirls about at night the city looks even grimmer than it is. A mate of mine called it Birmingham with skyscrapers, which is maybe a bit harsh. Nothing against Birmingham, I've only ever been there once to go to Villa Park, so I can't really compare the two.

But my point is that São Paulo isn't the typical Brazilian city, with endless beaches and girls in tiny bikinis and all that stereotypical stuff. It's the total opposite of Rio, for example, where it always looks boiling hot, happy and glamorous. Probably the best way to put it is that Rio is samba and São Paulo is heavy metal.

The night was cold and unwelcoming. Loads of *Corinthianos* were wearing woolly hats. Although the hardcore supporters wore woolly hats even in the summer. I never understood why. It looked daft. Not that you'd ever tell them that. Corinthians fans can be a bit intimidating. I don't want anyone to misunderstand. I'm not saying anything bad about them. They were the first supporters to raise their voices against the dictatorship in the 1970s. And then there was Corinthians Democracy a few years later, when Sócrates got the players together and installed this amazing player power movement that was a direct challenge to the far-right and the military rulers in power. How can you not respect fans like that?

But everything about Corinthians is hardcore. The club was formed by five factory workers in 1910 and their base is in the far east of the city, in the poor suburbs, although they have fans all over São Paulo, all over the country, in fact, and from all different classes and races. They are a bit like Liverpool in that respect. But that working-class ethic is still what defines them today. They're known as the *Time do Povo,* or the People's Team, and everything about them is the opposite of fancy.

More than anything, the fans demand 100 per cent commitment. And I mean demand. They give a louder cheer for the full-back who runs 50 yards to put in a crunching tackle or clear the ball into the stands than they do for the mazy winger who dribbles past five defenders and lays on a goal. That's the important stuff, that honesty and commitment, showing that you would do anything for the jersey. The club's fans are known collectively as the *Fiel,* the Faithful. The club motto should be 'No Frills'. Even the strip is as plain as can be: white shirts, black shorts. That aesthetic is their trademark. No mucking about.

Like all Brazilian clubs, Corinthians have their *torcida organizadas,* the organised fan groups. At

Corinthians the biggest was the *Gavioes da Fiel* (the Hawks of the Faithful). There was also *Camisa 12*, *Estopim da Fiel*, and *Pavilhão 9*, which was named after a cell block in Brazil's most notorious jail. Most of the *torcidas* have online shops, to sell their own merchandise to their members. Most of them have their own samba schools as well. Brazil, right? At the Pacaembu the *organizadas* stood behind the goal to the left, carrying big flags and wearing T-shirts with their torcidas' names on them. But they all stood a wee bit apart from each other, because there was sometimes friction between them. Kind of like social distancing before it was invented, but for ultras.

Corinthians were 1-0 up against River at half-time and the atmosphere was still buzzing. But it changed early in the second half. Marcelo Gallardo swung in a cross from the right and Corinthians' Dyego Coelho headed it into his own net. For a second there was total silence. Then the fans exploded in song like they usually do, showing their team they were still behind them. It's really cool that; it doesn't happen everywhere but it happens in Brazil. They feel this obligation to sing or chant right after they lose a goal. And there was still this sense that the tie wasn't over. Corinthians could still qualify with just one goal, because then it would be 4-4 and they would go through on away goals. But the truth is they weren't playing well and they conceded a second 15 minutes later when Gallardo, who had been the best player on the pitch by a mile, set up Gonzalo Higuaín to make it 2-1.

I watched it on YouTube again recently and the Brazilian commentator did that thing when he gives it the full 'GOOOOLLLL!!!!' when the home team score but does this half-hearted 'Goooolll!!!!' when the away team score. Like he's only doing it because he has to.

That was probably it for Corinthians because now they needed two more goals just to take the tie to extra time. Most people realised it was all over. And if they had fought back and gone down with a fight then what happened next probably wouldn't have happened at all. But they collapsed and ten minutes later Higuaín made it 3-1. There were eight minutes left and Corinthians needed four goals to qualify. They were out and everybody in the stadium knew it.

Right after River's third went in the trouble really started. All that pent-up tension that I've been telling you about just exploded. It was like the Corinthians supporters just snapped. Within seconds, there was a fan on the pitch trying to attack the Corinthians players. Three or four security guys ran on and grabbed him. A few seconds later there was another and then another. You could see them around the track, clambering up the fence that surrounds the pitch. Actually, lots of people were leaving too. They knew that things were going to get bad. But the ones that stayed were angry. And the guys trying to get on the field were really going for it. Sometimes a security guard would intercept them before they got very far. Sometimes a player would. One guy got right up to Betão, whose mistake led to River's second goal. Betão stood up to him, like he was ready for a square go there and then. He's a big lad, Betão, but still. Football players have balls of steel. How they put up with the abuse and the threats and the violence I'll never know.

And then it really all kicked off.

The fans charged down the terraces to try and get on the pitch. Big waves of them. I know I should have been repulsed. But I was awestruck. It looked amazing. Terrifying, mostly. But amazing in a crazy 'this is Latin American football at its worst' kind of way. I couldn't take my eyes off it. I still get a shiver today when I think about it. Like I said before, the hardcore Corinthians fans were always behind the goal to the left, either side of the big entrance where the art-deco letters spelt out Estádio Municipal Paulo Machado de Carvalho. The guys that had run down to pitch level were already massed under that entrance and they were charging the big green wire fence that surrounded the pitch. There were hundreds of them, pouring forwards. At first, there were about a dozen policemen inside the fence, battering it with their truncheons as the fans charged towards it and tried to climb over.

Then the crowd started shaking the gates. The fence had a big gate in it that could be opened to allow marching bands or people carrying equipment to come on to the field. The fans, hundreds of them, maybe thousands, were shaking the gates as hard as they could, trying to prise them open. The gates were fixed to the ground but one side came undone and the fans swung it open. There was a big cheer because now there was a huge gap for them to charge through and get on the pitch. But the police held them back. Just a dozen of them with their black truncheons, battering the fans, trying to knock them back and stop them from charging through the gates. Literally, knocking them back. They were totally outnumbered but they just kept swinging their truncheons as if their lives depended on it, which it probably did.

The police were heroes that night. They were totally outnumbered but they did what they had to do. If the fans had got on the pitch then God knows what would have happened. It was like they wanted to tear the Corinthians players limb from limb as some kind of punishment for losing. As if they had lost deliberately.

They were shouting that they wanted to 'Get Coelho!', who'd scored an own goal. Coelho had been subbed a few minutes before the third went in so he wasn't on the pitch when the fans invaded or he would have been in real danger. Poor Dyego Coelho. He's back at Corinthians now as their under-20 coach. Time is a great healer.

Missiles were also being thrown from the terraces, over the heads of the Corinthians fans and down on the police. Behind them, I could see dads shielding their kids from the flying sticks and bottles, trying to sneak behind the mob and out the ground. I saw people go down hurt. There's a famous photo from that night of a policeman holding his head and grimacing in pain under his big bushy moustache.

It seemed like every Brazilian football stadium back then was part stadium, part building site. They always seemed to be falling apart and there always seemed to be sticks and stones lying around. Maybe the fans were breaking off bits of the concrete terraces to throw at the police. It wouldn't have surprised me. Around about the same time, seven people died in Salvador when they fell through a hole in the top tier of the terrace that had been rotted away by years of beer and urine. The ground literally opened up below them and they fell to their death. In Recife a few years later Santa Cruz fans yanked a toilet from the floor of their Arruda stadium and threw it on a rival firm below. It hit some poor guy on the head and killed him. Imagine being killed by a flying toilet.

Once the police got organised they started firing these flashbang grenades into the Corinthians end. Have you ever heard a flashbang grenade go off? Those things are loud. They were designed by the SAS to disorientate enemies. The light is supposed to blind you for a few seconds and the noise is supposed to throw you off balance. They started firing those into the crowd. I couldn't believe it. All this inside a football stadium with the players on the pitch a few yards away. As all this madness was happening at one end of the ground, the referee, who had abandoned the match with six or seven minutes remaining, was at the other end trying to get the players off. He didn't have to ask them twice. The dressing rooms are below pitch level at the Pacaembu, under the stand behind the goal to the right. The tunnel down under ground is probably 30 or 40 yards from the terraces so there was no need for the riot police to hold their shields over the players or referee like they often do in Libertadores games. Nothing screams Libertadores louder than riot police on the pitch protecting players or officials from rocks, beer, gob and Lord knows what else.

Eventually police reinforcements arrived and the fans started to disperse. I remember wondering how I was going to get home. It was only a ten-minute walk. But doing that through masses of enraged *Corinthianos* and São Paulo policemen bent on taking their revenge didn't seem like a clever thing to do. So I used my press pass to run down to the dressing rooms. The Corinthians side was silent and the River Plate side was banging. I can't remember if they were singing or if they just had music playing but there was all this noise and a general atmosphere of joy. It was like they were having a wedding in one dressing room and a funeral in the other. I remember peaking inside the River dressing room at one point and seeing Passarella with a massive grin on his face, hugging everyone who came near him. Passarella almost never smiled.

The other thing I remember is standing outside and waiting for the Corinthians players to leave. At first there was a bunch of angry fans at the gate to the car park and they were waiting for the players to come out. The gate was about 50 yards from the entrance to the dressing room and the fans were there, shouting abuse and looking threatening. The anger hadn't abated.

The Corinthians players were clever. They just decided to wait it out. The match kicked off at 9.45pm and it must have finished about 20 minutes before midnight. By around 2am most of the Corinthians squad still hadn't appeared. They just waited for the fans to get tired of waiting for them. I can't remember how long it took for them to come out. I think I got tired of waiting. I wasn't writing about the game that night and the players obviously had no intention of showing their faces. They were holed up, like cowboys in an old western who had run out of ammo and were surrounded by Indians.

Elsewhere in the city, and I only found this out later, there were violent skirmishes. The police had to escort the buses carrying River fans away from the ground afterwards. Corinthians fans smashed up cars in the streets around the ground and a few went daft on the Avenida Paulista, the city's main street, smashing windows and stuff. There were clashes in other parts of the city. Quite a few people were injured over the course of the night, both fans and police. While all this shocked me, it didn't surprise me. Football is less violent in Brazil since the 2014 World Cup finals. Football is a bit calmer, generally speaking. Now they have all these new stadiums and exorbitant ticket prices. It's changed things a bit. But back then I went to matches in Brazil half expecting something horrible to happen.

Looking back, I know I should have happier memories of Brazilian football and I suppose I do. I've been to loads of matches, in the state championships, Série A, the Copa do Brasil, the Copa Libertadores, all that. I've seen games all over the country, from sold-out cup ties at the Maracanã, to indigenous league games in the Amazon, to local matches in front of a few dozen hardy souls in the middle of nowhere. I've been to World Cup matches, Copa America finals, friendlies, testimonials, everything. I've seen Ronaldo and Romário, Neymar and Ronaldinho, Tevez and Messi. I remember all these things. And I know I'm not supposed to say this, but all this stuff I just told you, that's what stands out. The craziness of South American football stands out. The intensity is something else. It really is another level.

Anyway, that's it. That's my unforgettable away day.

One Nil to the Arsenal
by Catherine Etoe

Umeå IK v Arsenal
UEFA Women's Cup Final
Umeå, Sweden
21 April 2007

It wasn't every day that Arsenal Ladies touched down to a flashbulb-popping reception from a gaggle of press and crowing pensioners offering words of wisdom about their upcoming opponents. But that was just the kind of welcoming committee that greeted the English champions when they flew into Umeå, on Sweden's eastern Baltic coast. It was fair enough; in two days' time the streets of this university town would be awash with thousands of football fans, all of them raring to go as the home team, Umeå IK, looked to gun down the north Londoners in the most prestigious club cup final in the women's game.

Getting to the northern-most reaches of Sweden had been a long haul that spring day, but apart from hearing defender Anita Asante declare that she could smell burning as the plane took off from Heathrow, the group had made for entertaining travelling companions. Their manager, softly spoken former professional footballer Vic Akers, had already come in for stick, swiftly earning the nickname 'The Surgeon' for his brilliant-white tracksuit top, while midfielder Jayne Ludlow's decision to don a lacy frock for a boot sponsor's recent photoshoot was clearly going to haunt her for some time.

Still buoyant by the time they arrived in Umeå, a few hundred kilometres from the Arctic Circle, Arsenal bore the attention from the waiting Swedish press and public with good humour too. Club captain Faye White diligently answered reporters' questions even though she was still not match fit enough to lead out the team; defender Yvonne Tracy merely smiled sweetly as one elderly lady declared, 'Ooh, you're going to meet Marta, she's the best player in the world.' Welcome to Sweden, where female footballers are front-page news and household names.

In all honesty, having often found myself without man, woman or beast for company in the press box while covering women's games over the years, all this attention made a refreshing change. As professionals and two-time UEFA Women's Cup champions, I knew Umeå and their star player Marta warranted it; as semi-professionals and the first British club to reach the final of this competition, I was sure history-making Arsenal deserved it.

They certainly got it in Sweden, Arsenal coming down for breakfast in our smart but unshowy city-centre hotel the next morning to find their faces splashed across several newspapers, much to everyone's amusement. Regional daily *Västerbottens-Kuriren* had even devoted four pages to the visitors, among them a spotlight on Dennis Bergkamp's golf buddy Akers, whose paid job was as 'Menocksamaterialforvaltare at Fredrik Ljungberg och de andrai I Arsenal FC' – in other words, kit man for Arsène Wenger and an international stable of Arsenal stars such as Sweden's very own Freddie Ljungberg.

With some less than flattering pictures accompanying articles that would take quite some time to translate, the ribbing kicked off again, but 'The Surgeon' avenged any mickey-taking at his expense by marching the squad to a nearby ice-packed lake for a mid-morning stroll. It was, as the saying goes, cold enough to freeze the nuts off a brass monkey. 'There you go,' Akers joked with physio

Claire Smith. 'You can get some ice from there – I'll hold yer ankles!'

After lunch for 25 at a local restaurant, it was back to the serious business of pre-match preparation for the opening tie of this two-legged final. Arsenal's chance to train on the artificial turf of the Gammliavallen Stadium was set for the late afternoon, while Akers and his captain Jayne Ludlow made an advance visit to the venue to serve up some juicy quotes for the waiting media.

Also there to greet them in the narrow pressroom that day was the trophy they had chased for five years. A curvy, question mark-shaped slither of bronze with an acrylic glass ball at its tip, the 40cm-high, 8.5kg gong had been perched tantalisingly close to the duo as they sat behind a long table at the far end of the room.

'I don't think I'm going to touch it,' Ludlow told me before the man from UEFA saved her the worry by whisking the glittering prize off the table and inviting Akers and his managerial rival, Umeå head coach Andrée Jeglertz, to grasp it for a photo opportunity. Recoiling like a kid coming face-to-face with a snake at a petting zoo, Akers was having none of it either. 'If you want to hold it, you hold it. I won't hold it,' the Arsenal boss chuckled as the two coaches prepared to pose for the photographers.

Looking relaxed on home turf, polo-shirted former Allsvenskan league professional Jeglertz appeared happy enough to oblige though, tightly clasping the metalwork in one fist while clutching Akers's hand in the other. Maybe the 35-year-old felt he could afford to kick superstition into touch; he had, after all, already held the trophy aloft as a champion in 2004, his first season at the helm of Sweden's premier side.

Despite delivering 24 major titles since 1992, Akers was yet to triumph on this stage and the 60-year-old, still wrapped up against the chill in his white club tracksuit top and blue jacket, was content to downplay his side's chances of beating Umeå. 'It'll be a tight game, tough game for us, we're playing against a professional set-up and it's going to be very difficult,' he said. 'They're going to want to go for the game, to try and put us out of the tie. Our aim is to stay in it, not to get beaten heavily. If we're still in the tie when we go back to England then it's going to be a super game next week as well.'

Had the Arsenal manager decided on his starting XI, the Swedish press enquired. 'Yes.' Would he name them? 'No.' What Akers would say was that his players were happy. 'We've been in good temperament,' he said. 'Lots of smiles and everyone's looking forward to the challenge.'

The challenge they faced was a phenomenal one. Yes, Umeå had seen leading lights Malin Moström and Anna Sjöström retire and Finnish international Anne Mäkinen had departed. They were also only a rusty two games into their own domestic Damallsvenskan season. But they had won both those matches and boasted two exciting new recruits in the golden ball and boot winner of the 2006 under-20 World Cup, Ma Xiaoxu, and Swiss wunderkind Ramona Bachmann. They could also call upon an experienced roster, including FIFA World Player of the Year Marta and her fellow Brazilian Elaine, World Cup silver medallists Hanna Ljungberg and Karolina Westberg, and Norwegian international Lise Klaveness.

With Umeå's training open to all that afternoon, I headed to the Gammliavallen pitch to watch these illustrious players warm up. For a few moments, there was a pram on the sidelines in front of me, the toddler inside sitting bolt upright and seemingly watching the team as keenly as I was. Umeå really were something else but that season Akers had concocted the finest Arsenal line-up I had seen in my eight years of covering the club, featuring as it did four national team captains, some prodigiously talented youngsters and a host of experienced internationals. Nine of the squad had recently helped England qualify for a first World Cup in 12 years. Carrying the baton of an unbeaten league run that had kicked off in 2003, the Premier League title was within touching distance, they had already added the League Cup to their bulging trophy cabinet and an FA Cup Final date was in the diary. The players juggled jobs with evening training sessions but still had an unprecedented quadruple in their sights in this, their 20th anniversary year.

Akers had been part and parcel of the club during every one of those years. Raised on the Essex Road in Islington, he was Arsenal through and through. He had grown up playing on the inner-city pitches at nearby Market Road, running out for boys' clubs in Camden and Shoreditch, and supporting the Gunners from the terraces at Highbury. He was a professional footballer in his 20s and had played at left-back with Cambridge United and Watford before joining Arsenal as a community liaison officer after eventually hanging up his boots.

Within two years he had brought a team he coached at Highbury's indoor pitch under his club's umbrella and, with men's vice-chairman David Dein as their president, Arsenal Ladies was born. It was 1987, an era of pay to play, when the game was run by the amateur Women's Football Association on a shoestring and league battles were drawn along regional lines. When a 24-team National League was launched by the WFA using Football Trust cash in 1991, two decades after the FA had lifted its 50-year ban on females playing on its affiliated grounds, Arsenal were placed in the eight-club Southern Division. They swept aside all-comers, winning promotion to the top flight as champions, while also defeating Premier Division outfit Millwall Lionesses in the League Cup Final.

The following season brought the real breakthrough. Arsenal retained the League Cup at Wembley Stadium, trouncing Knowsley United 3-0 ahead of the men's Third Division play-off final. The cherry on the cake, though, was doing the double over Doncaster Belles. Arsenal took the defending champions' Premier Division crown in a match that was sandwiched between a celebrity 11-a-side knockabout and a musical half hour from Aswad, all part of a benefit day at Highbury for injured boxer Michael Watson. They also saw off the England international-heavy Belles in the WFA Cup Final at Oxford United's Manor Ground. It was, Akers told me, 'one of the big turning points in Arsenal's history'.

While Arsenal carved out their place at the top table alongside Croydon, Doncaster, Everton, Liverpool and Millwall, Akers built his squads, seeking out up-and-coming players, bringing through youngsters and signing established winners. 'He just made you feel like he wanted you,' Faye White once told me, describing how she had signed in 1996 after Akers had driven to meet her for a cup of tea at Gatwick Airport and visited her parents. The deal was clinched when he took her to watch a training session at Highbury from the comfort of the executive seats.

His players may have been amateurs, but Akers was still a stickler for professionalism. There was to be no alcohol supped in club colours, opponents were never rubbished. Crowing in victory was not encouraged, grace in defeat was. Training under the lights at Highbury was morale-boosting, even if the high-intensity sprints had to be done around the pitch, never daring to touch the turf. Marathon speed sessions up and down the steps of the old stadium and full-throttle matches in the indoor ball court were hard graft. 'The way they applied themselves in those early years was phenomenal and that was really what kept me involved because I could see a future for the game,' Akers explained.

Arsenal already boasted six teams across the age groups, a centre of excellence and 12 major titles when I covered my first match as a cub reporter in September 1999. I can't remember the score and only recently realised that it served as a home debut for

17-year-old Casey Stoney, a future England captain and Manchester United manager. I do recall trundling around Boreham Wood FC's Meadow Park after Akers at full time while he busily tidied up the terraces and checked the locks. I told him my paper, north London weekly *Camden New Journal*, wanted to devote more space to his club. 'You'll be wanting my number then,' he replied, and I took it, his name still the first in my tatty black book of women's football contacts.

I only called when I really needed to, but Akers was a ready interviewee and a few days before the start of the 2006/07 season I had gone over to the Arsenal men's training ground at London Colney to speak to him and his new assistant Emma Hayes. A teenage left-footer for Arsenal in the 1990s, Hayes was stepping into the shoes of Akers's recently retired assistant Fred Donnelly as director of the Ladies Academy while also joining up with Mike Irving as first-team coach.

Hayes was a Spurs fan who had grown up kicking a ball around on the estates of Camden but had just returned from an award-winning five years in America bursting with ideas. 'It's the end of one era and the beginning of another,' Akers said. 'Hopefully it will throw a freshness into the week-to-week work we're doing and the girls will enjoy the change.'

It turned out that 30-year-old Hayes, who I had interviewed in 2001 when she packed in her job as a community coach with Camden Council to move Stateside, had even bigger aims. 'I'd like to push on in Europe,' she said. 'It's one competition we're capable of winning and the players feel that way. We'd like to get to a final and on a personal level this is the strongest team I've ever seen at this club so it's a realistic ambition.'

Hayes was right about the team. Over the years, Arsenal had lost players to retirement, other clubs or injury. But throughout it all, Akers had rebuilt, going that extra mile to land a special player, leaving the door open for a return if they had moved on and finding them jobs within the club or in the Ladies set-up where possible. As the season dawned, it felt as though he had finally come up with an ideal line-up.

Within the main group, six had joined in the 1990s. Four of them worked for the club: midfielder Asante, snapped up by Arsenal defender and development chief Clare Wheatley at a Ladies session in Burnt Oak aged 13; experienced Republic of Ireland skipper Ciara Grant, who left her homeland to sign in 1998; towering England skipper White; and world-class forward Kelly Smith, back after making her name as England's only professional in the Women's United Soccer Association

(WUSA) in America. There was also prolific striker Lianne Sanderson, a former youth player who debuted for the first team at 14; and England's most-capped active player at the time, winger Rachel Yankey, who had returned after spells with Fulham and Birmingham City.

Then came three turn-of-the-century signings: former Arsenal centre of excellence youngster Alex Scott, who was now established in the first team after a career-defining season away at Birmingham City where she switched from attack to defence; Academy medical officer Ludlow, considered such an awesome opponent that she had been voted Player of the Year by her Premier League peers three times since joining Arsenal; and Republic of Ireland number one Emma Byrne, team wit and a safe pair of hands with a half-century of caps.

Scotland skipper and PE teacher Julie Fleeting had arrived in 2004, cannily captured by Akers after her spell as a professional in America ended with the collapse of WUSA. An instinctive striker, her importance was underlined by the fact that Arsenal flew her down from Scotland for matches, with Akers ferrying her from the airport and back each time. Another welcome addition since 2004 was England international, football coach and mum-of-two Mary Phillip. A cup double winner with Millwall back in the day, the former captain of Fulham brought steel and speed to a defence that had just lost Kirsty Pealling to retirement after 20 years in an Arsenal shirt, but also featured no-nonsense England international Leanne Champ and stylish Republic of Ireland regular Yvonne Tracy.

The final pieces of the jigsaw were two new signings: Karen Carney, a fleet-footed England whizz-kid who had set tongues wagging as a 17-year-old with some barnstorming appearances at Euro 2005; and tough-tackling mother-of-one Katie Chapman, a fearless midfielder and England regular who was just 14 when she lifted both of Millwall's cups with Phillip, going on to play alongside the defender (and Yankey) as a professional at Fulham.

'Everyone brought something different,' Fleeting said to me years later. 'We had creative players, players willing to get stuck in and win the ball back, skilful players, we had a mix of everything and a great team spirit.'

By the time the season had kicked off, however, defenders Champ, Tracy and White were out with long-term injuries. The answer was to switch Grant and Asante out of midfield and into central defence, move Phillip to left-back and hand vice-captain Ludlow the armband. It worked a treat and, by November

2006, Arsenal were not only dominating domestically, they had finally got the monkey of two previously unsuccessful UEFA Cup semi-finals off their backs.

The only problem for this final was that Academy assistant director Kelly Smith was banned from playing any part. She was a talismanic player who could turn a game with the flick of either boot and had been compared to Zinedine Zidane by Dutch coach Vera Pauw during England's successful bid to reach the World Cup, a year-long campaign that climaxed in September 2006. Smith had turned on the style for club and country throughout and by the time Arsenal went into their semi-final away leg with Danish champions Brøndby that November, the 28-year-old was in the running for the FIFA World Player of the Year award. True to form, Smith bagged both goals for Arsenal in a 2-2 draw. Unfortunately, she was red-carded before the end of the tie and in the heat of the moment had flipped a finger at the jeering crowd and kicked a chair as she headed to the dugout. She was handed a three-match ban and would miss not just the home game against the Danes, but the two-legged final too.

Arsenal had pulled it off without their playmaker when they hosted Brøndby at Meadow Park for the return. Yankey, Carney and Fleeting steered the home side to a 3-0 win. They were roared on by a crowd of almost 1,300, among them a group of youngsters who were driven to the match in a minibus by their football coach, Arsenal's opening goalscorer Rachel Yankey. 'The player of the match for me,' Akers said of Yankey afterwards. 'She's realised she can do more for the team and I think she pulled it out today.'

Even so, with Smith in such superlative form, missing the chance to see her face-off against a world-class foe such as Marta in the final felt like a body blow for the sport. Underdogs for the first time this season, it was galling for Arsenal too, although they had the strength and depth to cope. 'We knew what we'd built between us as a squad and we were going to go out there and do everything we possibly could to win,' Phillip would later recall. 'I wanted that trophy in my cabinet.'

As they boarded the team coach for the Gammliavallen on Saturday, 21 April, it was all to play for. With a colour piece for *Fair Game (She Kicks)* magazine in mind, I had shadowed the team up to this point, but on the morning of the final I hardly dared even look at the players let alone make conversation, the weight of the occasion seeming too great for idle chatter.

The group were taking it in their stride, of course. On arrival at the stadium, Akers was fielding good-luck texts on his phone from the likes of Dennis Bergkamp. The yellow and blue seats of the Gammliavallen, home to both Umeå's men's and women's teams, were slowly filling up. Jeglertz had told me that around 2,500 people usually turned out to watch the women. For the final, 5,500 advance tickets had been sold with more expected to pay at the turnstiles.

With a mishmash of seating and standing areas, a wall of tall sinewy trees filling the skyline behind the lowest stand and an athletics track wrapped around the pitch, the Gammliavallen was not exactly a fiery cauldron. To my eyes it looked almost homely. Pictures of Umeå's stars, from both the men's and women's team, adorned the outside walls. A red bike stood propped against the main stand, a baby buggy hugged the front of a blue coffee kiosk in the middle of the long, single-tiered stand opposite. On the steep sweep of grass and woods behind, a small group could be seen enjoying a picnic away from the shade of the trees. To the rear of one goal, a line of fans stood in front of an art-deco-style hangar and a few parked-up coaches. Beyond the other stand a group of kids sat on piles of wooden pallets.

That said, by the time the 2pm kick-off was upon us, 6,265 spectators had filed through the doors. One man had brought a chunky drum. Many more had arrived bearing flags, most of them draped across the barriers of the main stand. It was a sea of black and gold, blue and yellow, red and orange. One bore the legend 'Umeå IK The Golden Stars', another was interwoven with the names of players – Elaine, Marta, Joanna Frisk, captain 'Karro' Westberg, Klaveness and Hanna 'Ljungan' Ljungberg; all were interspersed with the national flags of the squad, Switzerland's for Bachmann, China's for Ma, Norway's for Klaveness and June Pedersen, Brazil's for Elaine and Marta, Sweden's for the rest.

Teenagers Ma and Bachmann would start on the bench for this one, but when the team in black and gold took to the pitch, each clutching the hand of a young mascot, all their other big hitters were there. Arsenal's team sheet (in shirt number order) read: Byrne, Ludlow, Grant, Sanderson, Fleeting, Yankey, Scott, Carney, Chapman, Asante, Phillip. White, ever-present this season as an extra helper on match days, was nearing her return and named as a substitute, as were Champ and Tracy, while Gemma Davison and youngsters Gilly Flaherty, Sian Larkin and Rebecca Spencer completed the 18.

Their body language gave little away as they lined up alongside Umeå in the centre of the pitch. I later discovered that Ludlow, the Arsenal and Wales captain, had just delivered what several players would go on to describe as the pre-match speech of a lifetime. 'I remember her passion,' Yankey told me recently. 'She said, "You England girls will go to World Cups and Euros, this is my biggest game, this is my World Cup Final." She just went off on one and it was probably the best team talk we've ever had and needed, because we were under the cosh.'

There is no doubt that within the opening minutes Umeå ripped into the visitors. I was taking photos at the time, so I only made brief notes, but when I look back now the first mentions are mostly of Marta's tricks, flicks and near misses. 'The first 20 minutes we did have a bit of a panic and think, "Christ, these are good players,"' Ludlow would admit afterwards. 'Marta did me like a kipper once or twice.'

Yet even with the wind at their backs, Umeå were unable to get off the mark, constantly repelled by the solidity and fluidity of Arsenal's defence and keeper Emma Byrne's quick reactions. It wasn't all one way though, with Umeå having to cope themselves with a flurry of attacks down the wing from Carney, Fleeting and Yankey. A gap in play while injured midfielder Elaine received the stretcher treatment offered a chance to regroup and the entire Umeå team, goalkeeper included, gathered together presumably to discuss a way through. They had not found it by half-time nor after the restart, despite chances for Lisa Dahlkvist, Ljungberg and a gilt-edged opportunity four minutes from time created by the visionary Marta which substitute Bachmann struck over the bar.

Fleeting, Ludlow, Sanderson and Yankey threatened too, apparently urged on at half-time to test the keeper in the blustery conditions. Then, in stoppage time, they did exactly that. Asante broke up play in the middle of the park, Fleeting played the ball out to Scott on the right wing and the defender, taking two touches and still finding herself completely unmarked a good 30 yards out, let fly a looping shot that keeper Carola Söberg could only flap a hand at. 'I remember Ciara saying, "Five minutes, we need an away goal," and she was shouting at Jayne who was saying, "I'm trying,"' Scott told me the next day. 'I thought if I shoot and I miss it, Vic's going to go mad, but I thought why not?'

I have to confess that even with a stand full to the brim of stunned home supporters at my back, I whooped with delight when that goal came. FA national women's football development manager Rachel Pavlou remembers doing the same: 'We shouted and it was like a pin dropped; we had to sit down.' Scott celebrated pretty much where she stood, hand pointed to the air – right in front of the home dugout. Looking back at my photos, I can see Umeå's crestfallen bench with their hands over their faces while Jeglertz stood hands on hips in disbelief as every Arsenal player, including Byrne, instinctively mobbed their goalscorer. It was the 91st minute. There was no way back for Umeå after that. 'It was a tremendous shot, but we should be there, put pressure on her, but that's the way it is,' Ljungberg shrugged afterwards. 'It's going to be very hard for us in London, but we'll do everything we can to win the final.'

By the time Marta and co. arrived in Borehamwood eight days later, unbeaten Arsenal had won the league title with a 5-1 midweek thrashing of Chelsea with three games still to go. If they were weary, they did not show it; if they were nervous, they kept a lid on it. 'We were trying to get the players out of the dressing room and they weren't in a rush,' Hayes later told me. 'They were so relaxed and so confident in their ability to deliver.'

Akers had stuck with the same line-up as in Sweden, while Jeglertz had just replaced an injured Madeleine Edlund with Ma. The reception that greeted the teams when they walked out that Sunday afternoon was unlike anything I had ever seen at Meadow Park. With terracing that crept so close to the pitch it almost felt as if you could touch the players, this could be an intimidating place for visiting teams if enough fans turned out. They did; almost 3,500 of them flooded into the stadium and with the barriers surrounding the pitch awash on three sides with a tight line of fans, the younger ones in face paint, the majority in the red and white of Arsenal, the atmosphere was electric.

I honestly cannot remember the finer details of the 90 minutes that followed, I just know that I held my breath for longer than was probably healthy and Arsenal rode their luck for a similar amount of time. As expected, Umeå pressed and probed and fought for their lives. With every home attack and the cheers of the crowd came a powerful counterpunch, the visitors almost knocking Arsenal and their fans down and out with a string of chances as the clock ticked down. Once again, though, Arsenal's determination, the woodwork and heroic shot-stopper Byrne held firm. 'It was ridiculous really,' said Akers. 'The last 15 minutes they hit the crossbar, the post, the ball came off and hit Emma on the head and went wide; you are thinking, "How are we still surviving here?"'

But they did and with the score 0-0 at full time, that precious away goal from Sweden was enough to clinch the title for Arsenal. Then there were scenes: Sanderson tearful and euphoric, racing towards Akers and leaping into his arms; the team rushing to the dugout to celebrate as one; Ludlow finally putting her hands around that UEFA Cup trophy and waving it aloft on the podium with Asante while horns blared in the crowd and every player jumped around in sheer delight. There was no champagne in the changing room – Akers had been too superstitious to get any in – but nobody cared, the players rejoiced anyway, caught up in the thrill of the moment. 'We put a massive amount of effort into the game and we've got our rewards,' declared Akers. 'The result is ours and they can't take that away. What a year!'

Arsenal would go on to complete the quadruple that season, a record crowd of 24,529 fans watching them come back from a goal behind against Charlton to win the FA Cup. As I write in 2020, it is an achievement that has never been matched. When Akers stepped down as head coach in 2009, he had amassed 32 major trophies in 22 seasons, but this will always be the special one.

Soldiers Without Weapons
by James Corbett

Palestine v Thailand
2012 Olympic qualifier
Ramallah, West Bank
9 March 2011

In the gloaming on a freezing Ramallah evening, Sepp Blatter and Yasser Arafat peered down from billboards high above our heads. In international football's nexus, the first preliminary round of qualification for the Olympic football tournament between two minnows of the game would, in ordinary circumstances, scarcely merit interest. Beyond it lay a knockout round, group stage and play-off before passage to the London Olympics 16 months later.

But FIFA's Sun King and Palestine's late political giant would have understood intimately the symbolism of what lay ahead. Forty-nine years after the Palestinian football association's formation and 13 since it was formally recognised by FIFA, this game was the first competitive international match ever played on Palestinian soil. And everyone in Ramallah wanted to see it.

As hundreds of fans pushed their way through a narrow gate and made their way along muddy gangways to plastic bucket seats, caked in red soil and gravel, policemen disembowelled flags from their poles and searched supporters. The world was watching them today and nothing was left to chance. In the stands drums rolled and chants of 'Fil-a-stin, Fil-a-stin' filled the air. There was hope and expectation as the country stood on the edge of what was for most other nations commonplace, but for them unknown.

I moved with a fellow correspondent from the modest VIP area and press box and around the edge of the pitch to join the throb of the fans on the far side of the stadium. It was, as a colleague had said, where the stories were but I was torn. As a journalist, my heart always told me to follow the story, but we'd been explicitly warned not to leave the media area and had to argue and jostle our way past a phalanx of security officers to get there. We talked to fans in pidgin Arabic and broken English about their hopes and excitement. Many wore old English football shirts that we guessed had been donated via aid shipments. It was my first real time in and among ordinary Palestinian people. They sang to us, 'Fil-a-stin, Fil-a-stin.'

I was reminded that just a few years previously the Israeli Defence Force had used the same stadium to park its tanks. As I filled my notebook, suddenly the carefree mood ended, and the situation became frightening. A police line holding back throngs of supporters outside the stadium broke and the crowd surged forward, swarming through a narrow gap between the stands where they gained a glimpse of the pitch. However, the gates were locked and the vestibules packed. There was nowhere else to move. People started climbing up the sheer concrete walls of the stand, but the crush continued and I could feel the air being squeezed from my lungs. Then two small boys started crying and common sense took hold of the crowd. Amid the crush, bodies were angled to protect the boys who were lifted above our shoulders and bundled into the safety of the stands. The force of expectant bodies pushing up against each other lessened and we could breathe again.

I exited the crowd splattered in mud, my press pass torn from around my neck and ribs bruised. Gingerly I made my way back to the other side of the stadium and safety and awaited kick-off. In the main stand,

Mohamed bin Hammam, the president of the Asian Football Confederation and mastermind of Qatar's stunning bid to host the 2022 World Cup three months previously, eyed me as I made my way back into the main stand where he stood around the VIP area drinking heavily sugared tea. Hours earlier, as we'd sat in the lobby of Ramallah's Mövenpick Hotel, he had revealed to me his plans to challenge Blatter as FIFA president. He smiled as he watched me wipe the mud from my jacket. 'Did you get a good story, James?' he asked drolly.

* * *

For me, travelling to Palestine was always much more than about attending a football match. A decade earlier at the London School of Economics I had majored in Middle Eastern History and Politics and gone on to do the same in a Masters degree. I followed the reporting of great journalists like Suzanne Goldenberg, Robert Fisk and Don Macintyre in Palestine and was precocious enough to see myself following in their footsteps. I had worked as London correspondent for an English language Arab newspaper and shared pages with the great Palestinian thinker, Edward Said. I was filled with righteous anger as news bulletins and newspaper pages filled with stories of the second intifada while I sat powerlessly at home in London. I should be there, I told myself; I should be there. But I had a good life in London. I met my wife at university and was happily married at 24. I got a major book deal at the same age and bought a nice flat. I had lots of friends, a good life and interesting work. A few years later I became a father, but by then I knew I was never going to be the next Fisk.

The Middle East, meanwhile, spluttered from its age-old binary conflicts into a sort of insanity after the US and British invasion of Iraq. Al Qaeda and other militant Islamic groups turned a volatile and unpredictable region into a frightening and dangerous one, while journalists were sometimes seen as fair game for occupying forces. Not only was I not going to be the next Fisk, I wasn't sure I'd have wanted to be.

My fascination with Palestine and the Middle East hadn't originated from university or the newspapers though. It came from my maternal grandfather, Charles Mills, who had served in Mandate Palestine, Aden, Egypt and Somaliland as a young soldier in the Second World War and the years after.

Charles – or 'Didi' as my siblings and cousins called him – was born in 1924 and was my hero, as he was to my uncles and cousins. He was the finest man I ever knew. Indeed I do him a disservice when I say he made me the man I am today for I have never existed on the same level. But he showed me the person I should try to be.

There were three great threads that ran through his life: family, church and football, but really the boundaries between these were so blurred as to be indistinct. He worshipped at St Peter and Paul's Church in Crosby on a Sunday with the same people he went to see Everton with the day before. I was the fifth generation of Goodison season-ticket holders in our family, he was the third. On Sunday nights, I'd sit at his home drinking whisky and he'd tell me stories about Dixie Dean, Tommy Lawton and his own grandfather, a laconic Irishman who attended Everton matches in the 1890s. There was an unbroken line in our family that touched the start of our beloved Everton's history.

Didi was phlegmatic, philosophical, resigned to the sufferance that is the badge of all of the Everton tribe. He rarely stood to applaud a goal, no matter its significance or the bedlam that was unfolding around him. When Stuart McCall hit a dramatic last-minute equaliser in the 1989 FA Cup Final, his response of 'they'll still lose anyway' so enraged his best friend that punches were thrown between the two old men before their adult sons dived in to break it up. All his friends were Evertonians. I don't think it was a conscious decision and he never railed at the injustices suffered by the club. But he did see Evertonians as a distinct tribe. 'They're not like us,' he'd say about Liverpudlians. 'We're different to them. We're cut from a different cloth.'

Aged 14, in 1939, Didi saw Everton lift the title a third time, with the team of Ted Sagar, T. G. Jones, Joe Mercer and Tommy Lawton the best he had ever seen. Lawton, he said, was better than Dean, and even in old age he ran out of superlatives for T. G. Jones, the supremely talented Welsh international centre-back. And then war came and changed everything. In 1941, aged 17, he joined the RAF and didn't see home for six full years. He served as a navigator in bomber command in the Middle East. He seldom spoke of his war experiences and refused to collect his medals. Recollections tended to be defined by homesickness for his family and longing for Everton. Apparently one of his distant dispatches, about his memories of watching the flickers of light from the Bullens Road as cigarettes were lit up across the pitch by Main Stand patrons as dusk descended on Goodison, was published by the *Liverpool Echo*. But this was as close as he got to the journalistic career he once coveted. Plans for university were wrecked by the fighting. He left for the RAF as a boy and came back a man.

Within a year of his return he was married. Within two he was a father.

Instead of the newspaper industry, he followed his father to the wholesale market on Liverpool's Queens Square and spent his entire 42-year career working for the flower wholesaler, Charles White, rising to be a director. Many in the city's business fraternity knew him, and his presence in a melting pot where the city's merchant class rubbed shoulders with some of its poorest – and most unruly – denizens was in its own way a fascinating one. But still there was Everton. Awaiting him in Liverpool after he returned from the war was his 21st birthday present – albeit two years delayed. His first season ticket. He maintained it for nearly 60 years, belatedly sharing it with me, before I inherited it in the mid-noughties when he gave up on the match.

I loved my grandfather. I loved his decency, his humour, our shared interests: football, politics, history, religion. I knew he was incredibly proud of me too, of the books and the stories I had written, that I had fulfilled the career ambitions that had been left unmet by him. Even in my early 30s I had an elemental even childish desire to impress him. But writing about sport seemed too safe in comparison to the life he had led as a young man. I didn't know danger or the limits of human endurance. I lived a safe life, free from horror or threats; there was nothing particularly challenging meeting a footballer or a manager. So, while I was living out the career he himself had dreamed of, it seemed one only half fulfilled. And then I was invited to Ramallah to cover a football match and an awful lot changed.

* * *

At 3am on the day of the match I found myself in a windowless, strip-lit room in Ben Gurion Airport awaiting an interrogation from immigration staff. I had been travelling for 15 hours criss-crossing first London and then Europe before being ushered off to a side room shortly after disembarking my flight in Israel's capital. The room was empty but for a young woman in a headscarf and another English journalist who was headed for the match in Ramallah. One by one we were summoned to an interview room to be interrogated about our trip and our intentions. The border guards had taken exception to my BBC recording equipment and harangued me with questions for 40 minutes.

Football in Palestine, I learned after a few hours' sleep, had come a long way since the country's FA was effectively dissolved in 1948, following the creation of the state of Israel and the formation of the Israel FA in its place. The Palestine FA was reformed in exile in 1962 and recognised by FIFA in 1998 – virtually Sepp Blatter's first act as president. As ever, Blatter's decision was not without controversy. His critics said that you cannot have a national team without a representative state, but the FIFA president always promoted football as an agent for social and political change. A national football team is as potent a symbol of statehood as a flag or anthem and Blatter encouraged Palestine's nascent team morally and financially while the rest of the world turned its back.

Through the following decade Palestine was rocked by the second intifada, the collapse of the Oslo peace process, and repeated Israeli incursions into the Occupied Territories. But through it all, the country continued to play its international football, albeit in exile. In October 2008 the country's first friendly match was played in the same Faisal Al-Husseini Stadium, this time with Jordan, in front of the watching Blatter, but never had they played a competitive match until that March day.

'It's a long story,' Jerome Champagne, who until the previous year was one of Blatter's closest aides and was now working as an adviser to the Palestine FA, told me over breakfast after a few snatched hours of sleep. 'It's the story of a fight, of bureaucratic difficulties, it's the story also of kids loving the game and growing and playing in camps and the streets. The Thailand match is very important, not only for Palestinian football, but for the fight to create a Palestinian state.'

Over the next 48 hours I learned that the significance of the national team's return to home soil could not be overstated. In Ramallah, a sense of normalcy pervaded. You could buy a beer or watch a Champions League match in a shisha bar. There was a five-star hotel. There were no guns on show. Squalor and oppression lay a few miles away and the calm at that time rested on an uneasy equilibrium with Israel, but there I found a determination to show the rest of the world that despite everything, Palestine is normal. Football played an important part in that. 'Football is much, much more than just a game,' said Champagne. 'It was Bill Shankly who said that football is more than just a question of life and death. In this context, here football is fundamental for kids to have fun, to receive a form of education through the game, to have discipline, and all these things. But it is definitely much more than a game. That formula is sometimes used very often, sometimes wrongly, sometimes in exaggeration, but it is true here.'

A few hours later in the basement of our hotel, the Palestinian FA president, Jibril Rajoub, was holding court among a small group of journalists. A great bear of a man, he speaks in a curt, deliberate manner that demands your attention, thudding his fist against the table for emphasis. He simultaneously glowers and mocks and charms. That morning he told me that he hadn't slept in three nights, so busy was he getting everything ready for the game, and the strain showed across his weathered face. Someone whispered beforehand that he only ever met in basement rooms in case the Israelis tried to launch a drone attack against him. 'Politics has nothing to do with sport,' Rajoub pronounced, but then embarked on a 40-minute lecture telling us why sport was so fundamental to the Palestinian cause and intrinsically entwined with the country's political landscape. 'You will never meet a Palestinian [who hasn't had] involvement in some sort of direct or indirect political activities,' he admitted.

Rajoub was a senior figure within Fatah and once served as Yasser Arafat's national security adviser. When we first met some tipped him to be a future Palestinian president, but a decade on that hadn't happened. He had previously served 17 years in an Israeli jail for throwing a hand grenade at a convoy of Israeli soldiers. Whilst in prison he learned Hebrew and English and rose through the Fatah ranks on his release into exile in 1988. 'I was part of the resistance;

I was part of the freedom fighting. I suffered A LOT for my people,' he growled thudding his fist against the table again. 'I contributed a lot to my cause for it to be a success.' He said that violence is part of the past and that the Palestinian struggle has moved on. 'The world has changed,' he said. 'What was good last century is not suitable this century.'

One of Fatah's policies in the West Bank was to implement a bottom-up approach towards statehood, improving the quality of life and building institutions. The belief at the time was that by creating the greatest level of normalcy possible, the case for independence became irresistible. 'It is a rational decision for me, for the Palestinian political leadership to focus on this field and expose the Palestinian cause through sport, through football, through the ethics and values of the game,' he said. 'I do believe that it is the right way to pave the way for statehood for our people.'

With such high stakes imposed from the top, the burden of responsibility rested heavily on the young shoulders of the Palestinian Olympic team. But then few footballers understood their duties to their compatriots as inherently as Palestine's. 'We have 100 per cent responsibility to paint a smile on the faces of each Palestinian women, or boy or girl, wherever they are in this world,' said the defender Nadeem Basem

Barghot, pointing to the vast Palestinian diaspora. He claimed that Palestinians all over the world, including the dire refugee camps in Lebanon and Syria, would be tuning in to see them play. 'I consider the players to be soldiers without weapons,' he said.

Players on the national team were paid an annual stipend of $3,000 and put up in dormitories situated in the eaves of the national stadium. When we were shown around the player accommodations it was clear that they would be inconceivable to Europe's cosseted footballers. The conditions were basic, the rooms sprawled with dirty laundry and bedding, but the Palestinian FA were proud of how far they had come. Five years previously the same land where the stadium sat – which is now skirted by Israel's vast so-called 'separation barrier' – was used as a parking lot for Israeli tanks as they engaged in a major campaign of West Bank incursions.

Barghot told me that the 'main problem' facing the team was continued harassment and interference from Israel. For the Thailand match, Palestine's Tunisian coach Mokhtar Tlili called up a dozen players from Gaza, but only four were allowed to cross into the West Bank. 'We don't meet all the time and have proper harmony between the whole team,' said Barghot. 'Other problems are when we leave Palestine [for international matches] and the

Israelis don't give permission to leave. We need to wait for their permission before we decide who can play.'

The players are more circumspect when asked to talk about their personal struggles under occupation, shyly deflecting questions. Everyone is so focused on a good news story that there is little reflection on the death and despair that marks the lives of many Palestinians. According to the Israeli human rights information centre, B'Tselem, 6,330 Palestinians in the Occupied Territories had died at the hands of Israeli security forces in the previous decade.

'Every player in this squad will have lost at least one family member or know someone who has died in the conflict with Israel,' Champagne confessed to me on the bus to the stadium.

* * *

After all the hope and expectation, the match itself was almost anticlimactic. Palestine, trailing 1-0 from the first leg in Thailand, tore into their opponents but despite creating several clear chances lacked the craft and guile to score. Perhaps the absence of its eight Gazan players was telling. But it was one of those who had been permitted to cross between the Occupied Territories who made the breakthrough shortly before half-time. Abdulhamid Abuhabib struck a sweet

25-yard volley that soared into the top corner of the Thailand goal, sending the crowd into raptures.

Thailand clung on, however, and as wind and rain lashed the stadium in the second half, the players seemed to freeze. Hailstones pummelled the open terraces and the crowd began to thin. Thailand had a man sent off, but the breakthrough still didn't come. In the dying moments of normal time, Abuhabib sent a diving header wide with the goal at his mercy.

Extra time beckoned, and the temperature plummeted even further. As penalties neared, we were joined in the press box by an unexpected visitor. 'If it goes to penalties, I'll be too nervous to watch,' the Palestinian prime minister, Salam Fayyad, told me. 'I'll look the other way.' The weirdness of having a national leader turn up alongside me in the press box was heightened when a piper, who looked like Saddam Hussein albeit dressed in bright-yellow waterproofs like a trawlerman, also joined us and led the prime minister in a round of patriotic chanting. Abuhabib might have spared the PM the pain of a shoot-out but he sent a spectacular overhead kick over the crossbar in the last minute, and spot kicks followed. Both teams scored their first five kicks, but Palestine missed both their sudden-death penalties and Thailand prevailed 6-5. Afterwards the mood was bittersweet but there existed a belief that what had passed had a significance far beyond football. 'Today was a political victory, but I wish it was a football victory too,' said coach Tlili.

'The world now will see Palestine in different eyes, in sports eyes,' Rajoub told me. 'This is a new launch for the Palestinian people toward freedom and independence.'

Although later it turned out to be a footballing victory too, if only for a short while. A few days after the match the AFC kicked Thailand out of the competition for fielding an ineligible player. Sutjarit Jantakol, it turned out, had been suspended for one match after being sent off at an under-19 championship three years previously. It seemed harsh, and the Thai FA complained bitterly, but it was Palestine who went through to the next round against Bahrain. And it looked like Palestine might go further after winning the first leg 1-0 in Bahrain, and then going 1-0 up in the first half back in the West Bank. But two second-half goals for Bahrain saw them reach the next stage on away goals instead.

* * *

Some 48 hours later I was back home in my flat in London with my young family. By then *The Guardian* had run my report on the game in its main section and the BBC World Service had aired a radio package. My phone, switched off since departure lest I incur the exorbitant roaming rates, groaned with messages. The first one I picked up was from my grandfather, now aged 86. 'Looks like you've been to all my former haunts,' he said in his laconic Liverpool accent. 'Hope you wished the old country well.'

Seven months later he had a serious fall outside his home. Possibly only the cold air closing his aged arteries saved him from bleeding to death on the pavement. He was shunted from one nursing home to another; a shameful indictment of modern Britain, with its preference for privatised social services, who can discard those they don't want, and a shocking situation for a man who had fought for his country and devoted his life to helping others.

Slowly his senses, once so acute, deteriorated, but there were still moments when his face would light up. If I mentioned my name or one of his family it usually meant nothing, but the words 'Dixie Dean' always provoked a flicker of recognition. When I showed him the artwork for Neville Southall's book, which I was ghostwriting at the time, he unexpectedly announced, 'I know that ugly bugger!' I said my goodbyes to him in July 2012, when he was peaceful and calm. By complete coincidence, immediately afterwards, I had a meeting in one of the executive boxes at an empty Goodison Park. Having seen him so frail I had been unable to stop myself crying beforehand but being in the place where we had shared so many good times brought a sense of tranquillity. It's a privilege walking through the empty old stadium, just as it had been knowing and loving this great man.

He died a month later, but I wasn't sad, only very grateful to have known and loved him.

Although I went back, my work in Palestine was only a very brief interlude. However, it was one that made me think fundamentally about my career. So much of what I had done up to that stage was jobbing journalism. I wrote many good articles, but I also filled the pages I was told to do, rewrote stories off the wires, or rang in a footballer's clichés without really thinking too much about the wider significance of sport. But after the Palestine game I realised there was so much to be written about the intersection between sport, politics and national identity and so many stories left untold. I committed to be a better journalist, to be more thoughtful and selective in the work that I accepted or pitched for, that I might never be a Robert Fisk, but that my words could really matter, resonate and have an impact.

I was glad too that I went to Palestine – the first member of my family to do so since my grandfather's service – when Didi was still lucid enough to be aware of it. He kept a folded-up copy of *The Guardian* (although he bought other papers to get 'different perspectives', this was always his daily newspaper) with my article in it until the day of his fall. It was as if a circle had somehow been closed.

My grandfather died early in the morning of 22 August 2012. I was alone in my new home in Ireland and I drank whisky until I was drunk, put a note about his passing on Facebook, turned my phone off and went to bed. All my friends and most of my family were in a different country. At that moment I felt more alone than I had ever done in my life.

But other chapters soon opened. My brother texted me. He was in the Countess of Chester Hospital and his wife had just given birth to their first daughter. He thought I should be one of the first to know, and another thing, would I be her godfather? Julia is still too young to be fully indoctrinated in the ways of Didi: Catholicism, Evertonianism, gentle cynicism – but her time will come.

Saturday Night Lights
by Arik Rosenstein

Beitar Jerusalem v Bnei Sakhnin
Israel State Cup quarter-final
Jerusalem, Israel
25 January 2017

This is not a simple story. Understanding the meaning of this Israeli State Cup quarter-final match in Jerusalem requires context. That rainy January Jerusalem night wasn't just about progression to the next round. It was about complex identities, a very fluid and controversial concept everywhere, but especially in Israel. I will tell you my story about entering Teddy Stadium to sit between the supporters of Beitar Jerusalem and Bnei Sakhnin. But let's be very clear: my perspective is forever intertwined with my upbringing, as is every football experience. Regardless of the perceptions you may have about the Israeli–Palestinian conflict, and its peoples, you must remove the emotion from my experience to form your own opinions.

I was born in Long Island, New York in a small town called Lawrence. I am what society deems a modern Orthodox Jew. My upbringing was a sheltered and comfortable life. It was simple and easy to keep the Jewish laws in suburban New York. I was able to walk outside and find an abundance of kosher food, while knowing it was under trusted supervision. I walked around with a kippa, the Jewish skullcap, and never had any issues, until years later in a very different New York. I was able to keep the holy Sabbath that my family and I observed every Friday night until Saturday night. This cherished weekly tradition is when we shut off from all technology, and from the outside world, in an attempt to take a mental and physical break from the stresses of day-to-day life. It was great. I had everything I needed. I was comfortable.

As the son of an English expat, my childhood revolved around watching Chelsea matches while balancing the fixture list with my religious observance. This was problematic as the rules of Shabbat did not allow me to use any form of electricity during this time period. Yet in my house it was always understood; Saturday night, or *Motza'ei Shabbat* in Hebrew, was for football. We would watch recorded games that ended hours before, as if they were live. When the Jewish holidays came around, it could sometimes be three days before we were able to see a specific match. But that was the beauty of our little suburban, American bubble. We were able to see games that were being watched by millions globally, in an odd, Jewish-American silence that only we understood. And yes, watching Chelsea win the Champions League title in 2012 on a DVR recording that did not extend to record the penalties, nine hours after the game had actually ended, was an incredible moment for my father and I. Waiting for the internet to load the BBC's website was the longest five seconds of my life.

It's important to understand that we were attempting to balance the two deepest and most important aspects of our lives. Football and religion. It was never simple, when everything about these two – at least for me and my family – countered each other. On the few occasions we checked our phones while watching a match, my cousins in Israel, seven hours ahead, would often send messages and ruin the unknown emotion in a split second. Our post-Sabbath life simply did not resume until after the football had been watched on Saturday night.

This relationship, between my religion and football, is and forever will be incredibly complicated. In my younger years, certain lines would not be crossed. But as you grow up, your understanding of what you are born into changes. My religious lines became increasingly blurred. As I saw friends and work colleagues not adhere to the same Jewish observance, it confused me. Naturally, as a 12-year-old, Saturday nights were meant for football with my father and I. But when you get older, from 16 to 18, you start to form a very different view of the world and strive for different levels of independence. My friends, family, and experiences became less comfortable. People close to me were observing religion differently to me. That was when the lines began to blur.

It starts with the little things, such as staying in a hotel, and on Saturday morning you pass a television that has the match you were planning on watching that night. You feel a sense of saving time, that you don't need to watch the match on Saturday night any more. You begin to feel more in sync with the world. These moments where your temptation of simply looking, counters everything you are taught. Then it becomes humanised. Your friend, who is also religious, tells you to sit down on the couch. We will 'watch and not tell our parents'. Rather than viewing religion as a part of your own life that you intrinsically believe in, it becomes something else, something that is part of your parent's expectation of your life. I never chose this path. I never saw what it was like to spend every weekend with my parents and grandparents in Borussia Dortmund's 'Yellow Wall'. I was in synagogue, every Saturday, praying to God. To a God that I am not sure I believed in.

The struggle then progresses when the conversations with family closest to you begin. It turns to loopholes, where you pretend to 'think out loud' and proclaim, 'Wow! I wonder what the Chelsea score is?' hinting at your non-observant grandparents to turn on the television. The logic is simple. According to Jewish law, one is not allowed to ask of another Jew to desecrate the Sabbath. By me asking my grandparents, fellow Jews, to turn on the television – it is a direct desecration of the Sabbath. But, if they somehow 'decide' to turn on the match under their 'own influence', then I am technically not breaking anything. And I can go on with my Sabbath, 'morally'.

You see, what we tell ourselves is often flawed, but it's those flaws we choose not to see. My religious observance took on flaws that I knew existed but was not willing to see. I was starved of a football culture my whole life, but the truth is, I *did* grow up in a form of football culture. It was niche, but it very much existed. The difference is, I never felt the feeling of being 'normal', of being included, I just felt it was impossible with my religious observant lifestyle.

Now, you are probably assuming that I hate this struggle. The opposite is true. The concept of religion can often feel constraining, but I have grown an appreciation and understanding that I can be a part of the football world as an observant Jew. I began to realise this possibility at the age of 18. But only after I felt I had this 'authentic' experience I sought. After graduating from my Jewish high school, my next step was quite common in my culture. I took a gap year before university. The idea was to experience a freedom of 'no responsibilities' and exponential mental growth. Most of my friends went to US-centric programmes, while I enrolled in an Israeli leadership development programme that conveniently was located a ten-minute bus ride from the local football ground, Teddy Stadium, the home of Beitar Jerusalem. The idea was to attend as many matches in person as possible. That was the 'growth' I sought.

The experience was surreal. I went from watching recordings of Chelsea matches hours after the Sabbath to attending a match every three days at Teddy. I got to know the security guards, food vendors, bus drivers. I finally had the experience of local football I had sought all these years. The matches were rarely on the

Sabbath, and the football was surrounded by many different, religiously observant people. But I wasn't prepared for the cultural gap when Beitar Jerusalem and Bnei Sakhnin played, a fixture that has a history of violence, racism and pain.

Beitar Jerusalem emerged from the revisionist Zionist movement founded by Ze'ev Jabotinsky, promoting a more muscular, right-wing Zionism. The club draws its support traditionally from the political right, especially Israel's Mizrahi and Sephardic communities, Jewish communities with roots in the Middle East and, before that, the Iberian Peninsula. In the decades after Israel's founding they were very much on the periphery as cultural and economic power was held by a left-wing Labor party dominated by the Ashkenazi, Jews with European roots. The club has strong links to the Likud party and is renowned for perhaps the most racist ultra group in world football, La Famila, who have refused to countenance the idea of an Arab or Muslim ever wearing its famous yellow and black shirt.

Bnei Sakhnin, meanwhile, is Israel's most successful Arab club. More than 20 per cent of Israel's population is Arab, a constituency that has become increasingly marginalised in recent years. But Israeli Arabs also play for the Israeli national team and still broadly have greater economic and political rights than Arabs in neighbouring countries. The Qatar government famously paid for the renovation of their Doha Stadium and the team, and its red shirt, has become a symbol for the Arabs in Israel. But when the two clubs meet sparks always fly. Before the 2016/17 season, the Israeli league decided to ban away fans when Beitar and Sakhnin played. I was naturally quite upset not to be able to experience a rivalry that was said to define the region. I had always read that it was the fiercest in world football.

But then, a few days before the State Cup meeting between Beitar and Sakhnin, the Israeli Football Association released a statement. There would be a trial for future seasons, allowing travelling Sakhnin supporters into the Teddy Stadium. It was part of ongoing efforts by both clubs and the FA to kick racism out of the game. My eyes lit up. I understood this was going to be historic for Israeli football and I was going to be there.

I messaged the football WhatsApp group that I formed with friends from my programme. My Scottish friend, Eddie, decided to come with me. This was not something I wanted to experience alone. I had no idea what the policing and safety precautions would be. My only sources of research were the countless books I read about hooliganism, and the past incidents that overshadowed this fixture.

The game was to kick off at 7pm on a Wednesday. I remember distinctly the buzz around my neighbourhood, the affordable housing projects of Gilo Alef. It was a working-class neighbourhood. The area is often demeaned for being filled with *arsim*. The closest equivalent are perhaps English skinheads; young men wearing expensive tracksuits with outlandish buzz cuts. Israel can almost be as class obsessed as British society, and it is a big insult to call someone an *Ars*. I have met and befriended *arsim* – it is a complex and fluid identity. You have people who dress like *arsim* but don't speak or act like them, and you have those that act *Ars* but do not look it in the slightest. Beitar Jerusalem fans, specifically the infamous La Familia supporters, are described negatively as *arsim*.

I found myself walking to the local community centre, Beit Matanya, passing by many homes of Beitar supporters discussing the *milchama* – or war – that will occur that evening. It felt as if the entire neighbourhood was preparing for an attack. The local supermarket closed early as the two brothers who owned it were Beitar season-ticket holders.

I finished my weekly chores, of making dinner for the 60 people on my programme and found myself with 30 minutes to get to the stadium. Every bus was filled with Beitar Jerusalem supporters, so I found myself sprinting to the stadium, past a line of vehicles with Arabic adverts, and one regular public bus filled with Sakhnin supporters dressed in red. This was really happening.

Teddy Stadium is surrounded by sand and dust. As the rain fell it was transformed into a sea of mud. I wanted to see everything that I could about what this derby means to these supporters. The way the fans entered the stadium, smoked their cigarettes, how they angled and shelled their sunflower seeds. It all mattered. I needed to see and feel it all.

I found Eddie, standing there calmly by the entrance. We walked in and I heard the whistle blow, followed by intense drumming. The Beitar supporters started screaming, 'war, war, war' in Hebrew. I had just entered a political conflict that was being played out on the football pitch.

Eddie and I knew exactly where we wanted to sit. While the stadium was packed, we found our seats in the spot closest to the away fans. As we walked past La Familia's section, the sunflower seeds, cigarettes and flags were put to the side. The singing was so powerful, the edges of my fingers were vibrating. It was much more than supporters losing their voices, it felt as if their vocal cords were slowly tearing apart. I understood that this had become much more than a right-wing team against an Arab team. This was about the very essence of identity.

As we arrived to our seats, I immediately looked to my right and saw the Bnei Sakhnin supporters. The section was covered in red flags, with the occasional Palestinian flag. Each challenge was intense and powerful. Daniel Eibender made it 1-0 to Beitar Jerusalem in the 41st minute. The screams were infectious. Everyone was jumping around and celebrating. When I looked around, the fans in my section didn't congratulate each other. Rather, they turned towards the Sakhnin supporters and started singing a song that has since been banned.

They started singing 'Mohammed *meit*', which translates as 'Mohammed is dead'. My eyes widened in complete shock. As someone surrounded by fellow Jews, believers in God, I asked myself, 'Was this really happening?' Let's be clear, it wasn't everyone singing. But it was a substantial section. I found it hard to believe, after all my people have been through, after my life of confusion with God, that this could happen. My fellow Jews, directly insulting another religion's beliefs. But it was real, this idea that football could incite further hatred and polarisation.

The disappointment continued. Itay Shechter doubled the lead 71 minutes into the match. He decided to celebrate in quite a controversial way. Rather than celebrating with team-mates he went into the crowd and took a supporter's kippa and prayed loudly and emphatically, adding to the religious tension already in the stadium. The Beitar supporters loved it. Shechter was a player who understood what it meant to them. The intention was clearly to agitate. Everyone knew that.

Each section was covered with a heavy police presence. It was excessive, but for good reason. When Bnei Sakhnin got a goal back, the atmosphere became more hostile. As I looked to my left, Eddie was sitting near a teenage Beitar supporter who began shouting racist taunts. A steward with a covered face heard this and gave the supporter a warning to calm down or he would find himself out of the stadium. The supporter then turned his attention to the steward with this mask. The supporter, on hearing his Arab-accented Hebrew, started directing the racist slurs at the steward. The steward angrily grabbed the teenager's shirt and warned him to stop or he would get hurt. Other supporters saw this and got involved before the steward was taken away by his colleagues. The impact on me was twofold. The steward's entire face was covered except for his eyes. We know why. It reminded me of not being able to walk around New York City with my kippa for fear of anti-Semitism. The match finished 2-1. Beitar had won.

I left that stadium sad. Demoralised. Ashamed. But then I realised there is more context here. All the nations, money and power in the world tried to get these groups together to discuss and respect a bigger picture. The only thing that has successfully done that is football. It is often said, football shouldn't be involved in politics. I have learned to reject this flawed notion. The two are inexorably connected, and always will be, whether the away fans are there or not.

The Georgian Crossroads
by Steve Menary

Lokomotiv Tbilisi v Dinamo Tbilisi
Tbilisi, Georgia
11 March 2017

Drinking crushed pomegranate juice from a street market trader watched over by the Mother of Georgia was an unusual pre-game drink. The pomegranates had been sliced in half and stacked on a wooden trestle table with a portable crusher clamped to the side. The halves were crushed, leaving a husk that was thrown away. There was an easy analogy to be drawn with Georgian football, which like the pomegranates had been squeezed dry by forces beyond their control and left to rot.

Visiting Tbilisi had been an ambition since Dinamo Tbilisi – the then champions of the USSR – thrashed Liverpool 3-0 in Georgia to send Bob Paisley's side,

European Cup holders and winners for the last two years, out in the first round in 1979. Back then, the Union of Soviet Socialist Republics was a dour, mysterious monolith for most young football fans but Dinamo succeeded in partly smashing that aura.

A side full of Georgians led by the elegant David Kipiani, whose dribbling would prove so inspirational to his compatriots over the years, cruised home watched by a boisterous home crowd of between 90,000 and 110,000 people. Alan Hansen was caught on the edge of Liverpool's box by the elusive Kipiani, who created a chance that Vladimir Gutsaev tapped home. Liverpool's defence was then torn open as Giorgi Chilaya charged down the field and Ramaz Shengelia lobbed Ray Clemence for a second. A penalty from Aleksandre Chivadze sealed a humbling night for English football's finest.

A 6-3 aggregate defeat to German champions Hamburg followed in the next round, but most of that Dinamo side went on to lift the UEFA Cup Winners' Cup in 1981. Though Dinamo won a dour final against Carl Zeiss Jena of East Germany and could be underwhelming against other European sides, a 4-1 savaging of West Ham at Upton Park in the quarter-finals sealed an enduring mystique for some British fans.

Time, and the break-up of the USSR in 1991, has subsequently not been kind to Dinamo or Georgian football. As communism collapsed, corruption, gangster capitalism and organised crime all took their toll. Football has survived – just – but the sport's role as a national sport now faced a different challenge.

Football's all-pervasive presence is often so powerful that its assumed role as the national sport across the globe seems unquestionable, but not always. Other sports manage to flourish and challenge football's omnipotence. In Georgia, the biggest threat to domestic football – apart from foreign leagues on TV and some of the people who have run the game – was rugby union. The Georgians' appearance at the 2015 Rugby World Cup was a fourth successive qualification and their showing in England – two wins from four games – guaranteed automatic qualification for the next event in Japan in 2019.

Georgia were not the first Eastern bloc country to try and match the established rugby powers from Western Europe. When Dinamo were showing what Georgian footballers were capable of in the 1970s and early 1980s, Romania had challenged the Western elite at rugby. Inspired by contact with the French in the early part of the last century, Romanian rugby flourished and by the 1980s the Oaks had beaten

Scotland and Wales, and only narrowly lost to England 22-15 at Twickenham, a game I had been at with my rugby-loving dad. Had Romania been admitted to the old Five Nations perhaps the game there might have had a different trajectory but accepting a communist country with a political leader like Nicolae Ceaușescu was anathema to European rugby bosses.

Instead, an Italian team that continues to struggle was admitted when the competition belatedly expanded in 2000.

By 2016, Georgia was at the same point, the fortunes of football and rugby at a crossroads: one on a seemingly interminable slide, the other surfing a wave of enthusiasm. Pitching two separate stories to the BBC World Service, who were understandably keen on value for licence fee-payers, I suggested two angles: one on the fall of Georgian football and another on the rise of the country's rugby side.

The initial trip was cancelled at the last minute due to a family illness but, in November 2016, Georgia's rugby union team were staying in Edinburgh prior to a game with Scotland in Kilmarnock. Staying with family in Glasgow, I met Georgia's national coach Milton Haig to discuss rescheduling. 'Come for the Russia game,' said the diminutive, laid-back New Zealander. 'You'll see nothing quite like that.'

In 2008, two parts of Georgia, Abkhazia on the Black Sea and South Ossetia in the South Caucasus, rose up to claim their independence. Georgia tried to stand up to the Russian-backed separatists but were humiliated. A ceasefire prevailed, and hostilities were then confined to sport, which usually brought about a Russian victory. With one exception: rugby. Georgia's rapidly improving side were simply far too good for the Russians and the fixture had now become the country's biggest sporting occasion.

The game in the Rugby Europe Championship was on the second week of March, which was also the same weekend that Dinamo were due to play their historic rivals in Tbilisi, Lokomotiv, in the local Erovnuli Liga. I could take in Tbilisi's oldest derby and the most heated sports fixture in Georgia at the same time.

* * *

Getting to Tbilisi was easiest via Istanbul, which is often seen as the gateway to Asia although Georgia is further east. Iran and Iraq are due south and depending on the time of year, the time difference with the UK can be four hours. Few places in Europe can feel as far away from the UK as Georgia.

In Tbilisi, the Mother of Georgia towers above the Georgian capital. Sword in one hand, bowl of wine in another, the statue is supposed to symbolise the hospitable and valiant nature of Georgians and was built in 1958 to celebrate the 1,500th anniversary of Tbilisi. The valiant but failed recent wars with the Russians also produced a monument in the shape of bow-shaped glass and steel Bridge of Peace, which was built in 2012, but football has also been used to try and recover what has been lost.

FC Tskhinvali had been based in Gori in what is now independent – but unrecognised – South Ossetia. A new club was founded as a political ploy to assert Georgian claims to the breakaway state. After winning the second tier Pirveli Liga in 2013, the club qualified for the 2015/16 Europa League but with few fans and dwindling financial support, FC Tskhinvali – like much of Georgian club football – had started to unravel.

After meeting Milton Haig again and some of the Georgian rugby players (of which more later), David Tsabadze from FC Tskhinvali agreed to pick me up outside the squad's training base. A decade earlier, the Shevardeni Stadium had been home to a football side but rugby moved in. David was short, unshaven, with sunglasses constantly perched on his balding head and squeezed into a leather jacket that was never going to button up. He leapt out of his old car and I squeezed into the back with two of David's associates, neither of whom spoke English. My understanding had been that Tskhinvali were playing at Meshki Stadium in Tbilisi. 'No, no,' said David, his seat belt looking dangerously close to breaking as he leant round to speak. We were in fact setting off for the city of Rustavi, around 16 miles from Tbilisi. 'At Meshki it's 1,000 Lari [about £230] for one game but in Rustavi we get three matches for that price.' Later, after the FC Tskhinvali game, I mentioned to a contact at the Georgian federation that the game had been moved. No one seemed to have known.

Our car barrelled out of Tbilisi, passing Soviet-era housing blocks in the middle of nowhere and people selling drying meat on the sides of the street. The driver was keen on overtaking and gunned the engine looking for power that didn't seem to be there. Each time we just dodged the oncoming traffic and slipped back into our lane. We reached Rustavi, where we drove down a hill into a virtually empty Stadioni Poladi.

The lack of spectators for Tskhinvali's game with Merani Martvili was no surprise. There was the sudden switch of venue, of course, but also the fact that the match was being played on a Friday afternoon. Playing at night might have boosted the attendance but the absurd economics of Georgian football ruled that out. 'No one plays under lights; it costs too much,' said David. 'And no one charges for tickets.' But the players are all full-time? 'Yes,' nodded David eagerly, seemingly oblivious to the absurdity of the economics of football at this level.

Some players were on as little as £40 a month, and apparently full-time. But that was not a living wage. Leading players in the top flight averaged around £2,000 a month according to the local players union, although foreign players, particularly from Africa, were paid less, often closer to £1,000. Low and late payment remained a problem which meant that match-fixing was endemic in Georgian football. At least ten games had known to have been fixed in the previous three years according to the Georgian Football Federation, although the true number is likely to be far higher.

There was certainly little evidence of money in Rustavi, where fading, curling photos of glory days gone by, of trophies won and victories celebrated by FC Rustavi, the ground's main tenants, were pasted all over the office. Old photos bent off the wall, obscuring the faded and washed-out images of times long forgotten. Among the photos were cuttings from Dinamo's 1981 Cup Winners' Cup victory. Even here, among FC Rustavi's achievements, Dinamo's glories had a place.

By the time kick-off arrived in Rustavi, a few dozen people had traipsed down the hill into the ground. Cigarette butts and the husks of sunflower seeds soon began to pile up on the floor, although there was nowhere to buy either. Not only were there no shops but there had not been any South Ossetians at the club for the last six years. In fact, Rustavi was even farther away from South Ossetia than Tbilisi was. The football drew little response from those in attendance as Tskhinvali lost 3-1, their only goal a late and uncelebrated consolation.

Back in Tbilisi I met with Nika Jgarkava, vice-president at the Georgian Football Federation. Bearded, bald and full of life, Jgarkava joined the GFF two years earlier and was involved in sweeping changes. We met in a bar selling German lager with Bayern Munich memorabilia on the walls. Identifying the reasons that Georgian fans were falling out of love with their clubs was not hard. The Bundesliga's FC Hollywood were, along with Spanish giants Barcelona and Real Madrid, the biggest teams in Georgia, where the clubs existed – or subsisted, really – in the slipstream of these modern super clubs.

'If people don't have a feeling that the club belongs to them, then it's very difficult to make them think that the club does belong to them,' says Jgarkava. 'You have to go back to Soviet times. Then everything was state-funded. After the Soviet Union was gone, in order to sustain football the state had to continue to subsidise the sport otherwise it would have gone. Not completely, but down to a grassroots level. Maybe if we did that at that time, maybe it wasn't such a bad thing.' Jgarkava trails off.

After independence, Dinamo was briefly renamed Iberia Tbilisi – the first of many steps towards alienating its old fanbase. The original name was reclaimed but success abroad became an increasingly distant memory. After Georgian businessman and politician Badri Patarkatsishvili bought the club, Dinamo did reach the group stages of the UEFA Cup in 2004 and faced English opposition again. After losing 2-0 to Newcastle United at St James' Park, Dinamo's campaign dwindled, ending with a 4-0 hammering at home by Portugal's Sporting and a 5-2 thrashing in Greece by Panionios. Businessman Roman Pipia took control in 2011 and two years later, Dinamo reached the play-off round of what was now the Europa League but were crushed 8-0 on aggregate by Spurs.

Dinamo become a monolith in Georgian football. The club had excellent facilities and more money than all of their rivals combined but their fanbase was dwindling. In 2015, Dinamo's budget had been estimated at £18m. This was equal to the combined budget of the rest of the league. UEFA's Financial Fair Play rules do not apply to clubs with annual revenue under €5m and every Georgian club bar Dinamo was exempt from FFP. 'When I talk about Georgian football, I don't talk about Dinamo,' says Bakar Jordania, the GFF's head of licensing. 'They are totally different. They are managed like a mid-sized European club.'

Dinamo were the only club to charge entry but two Lari per head – less than 50p, from attendances that often slipped below four figures – was certainly not paying the wages of many players. European football and the UEFA money it brought was increasingly important at clubs which had often come back into public ownership. In a 16-team top flight, only Dinamo, Dila Gori, Lokomotiv, Saburtalo and Torpedo Kutaisi were funded privately. Torpedo Kutaisi had been owned by Georgian petroleum company Wissol but they handed the club back to the local council after discovering that local football was a money pit. In the second tier, only Merani, WIT Georgia and Gagra were classified as privately owned but that could be misleading. A club with ten per cent of funding from outside sources and the balance from local councils or government-controlled corporations would be described as privately owned.

'Because clubs are privately owned does not mean there is good governance,' adds Jordania. 'We have privately owned clubs that also want money from the government. And clubs that are owned by private individuals [but] do not have links with the local community.'

In 2015 a new administration at the GFF began looking at a different ownership model. FC Hollywood were not the only Germans to make an impression in Georgia. Impressed with German football's fan-centric 50+1 ownership model, the GFF wanted to start again. In 2017 the top division was cut to ten clubs with the state giving each club one million Lari (around quarter of a million pounds) and then offering to match funding from private investors up to 500,000 Lari.

In addition to persuading the government to use up taxpayers' money to bail out professional football, the season was also radically altered. With so many clubs reliant on money from public budgets, which were set annually and not always agreed by the time that the regular European season kicked off, Georgian sides were at a disadvantage when qualifying for UEFA competitions begun in July. 'Before, when our clubs were playing in European qualifying, it was at the start of our season,' Jgarkava explained. 'Because most of the players are on one-year contracts, we are not in a good position. Managers don't know their team. Now, when we play in Europe, we will have settled teams.'

Since 2017, the season now begins in March and ends in November but there seemed little eagerness as Lokomotiv played their second game of the new season. After beating Dinamo Batumi at home, Lokomotiv returned to their Mikheil Meshki Stadium for the oldest top-flight game in Tbilisi. Lokomotiv was formed in 1936. As the name suggests, the club was connected to Georgia's railways but the club had managed little success since independence and the recent impetus was with Tbilisi's third top-flight club, Saburtalo.

Saburtalo are from the central district of Tbilisi and were founded in 1999 by Tariel Khechikashvili, yet another Georgian businessman who used football as a platform to enter politics. Saburtalo's own Bendela Stadium had a tiny capacity. Like Lokomotiv, the club also played at the Meshki, named after the dazzling Georgian winger Mikheil Meshki who played for Dinamo and Lokomotiv.

Dinamo own their stadium, the vast Boris Paichadze Dinamo Arena where Liverpool were vanquished, but the GFF own the Meshki. Lokomotiv were paying them 3,600 Lari (a little over £800) a game for the privilege. But, as usual, there was no gate fee. If a product costs nothing, then – some economists would argue – it has no value and there were precious few fans who had come to see Tbilisi's oldest derby. The pomegranate sellers had long since disappeared, targeting Tbilisi's tourists rather than any trickle of supporters on their way to the Meshki's smart new 25,000 capacity bowl. Outside the ground there was a replica of the Cup Winners' Cup won by Dinamo in 1981. Paving slabs were decorated with names of famous players from Kipiani to Giorgi Kinkladze, yet another Georgian famous for dribbling whose skills took him to Manchester City, but none of this drew any attention from the handful of fans walking past. Those days were gone, long forgotten.

Inside, the seats were a mix of white, yellow, blue and red. At a glance, this created a sort of optical illusion of a fuller ground but there were only a few hundred fans dotted around. The crowd had been smaller in Rustavi, but that was for a neglected club formed as a political protest that simply appeared to be fulfilling a fixture in a dilapidated stadium. The game at the Meshki was a derby between Tbilisi's two oldest clubs, one of which had lifted a European trophy. In the executive suite Lokomotiv's president Lexo Topuria somehow maintained his optimism.

'In the past, we were financing on our own so it's a big welcome that the government is providing this support,' said the tall, casually dressed Topuria. 'This is our biggest problem. Since the break-up of the Soviet Union, we had only one great team, which was Dinamo Tbilisi, and everyone thinks in the past. We need some success for people to come to the gates.'

That success lies, said Topuria, in taking players abroad. 'There is potential there,' he adds. 'It's like an export for Georgia. If you take wine or nuts, football can also contribute something to this export.'

At the Meshki, there is little to attract likely buyers to players from either Dinamo or Lokomotiv. The more muscular Lokomotiv side win a desultory game through a 57th-minute goal from their diminutive Russian midfielder Nodar Kavtaradze. No one playing at the Meshki that day looked likely to get their name engraved on a plaque outside.

Between 2013 and 2016, Dinamo had won three titles and signed big-name players on up to £4,000 a month to make the European group stages but failed to get any further. The strategy changed. Younger players on wages of around £750 a month were recruited with offers of bonuses and incentives but there was none of the flair or excitement provided by Kipiani or Kinkladze on offer or any of the other Georgian legends of yesteryear. The pastries, coffee and half-time chat provide the biggest smiles.

In countries where corrupt governments have control, some people choose to live parallel lives; living alongside rather than in opposition to the state. Wearied by the state of their own club game, supporters in countries like Georgia are increasingly becoming parallel fans, following football but not their own. International success can, like the clubs in the old days of the USSR, provide some succour but, once lost, support is hard to win back if there is an alternative on offer. 'Football has a long history,' says Beso Abashidze, head of Georgia's fledgling players union. 'In reality, we don't succeed as a national team. In terms of popularity, it's football at the moment but in five years I don't know. I think more children choose rugby than football because of results. The children see our team winning, they qualify for three World Cups and also the next one.'

* * *

A day after the desultory Tbilisi derby, there is an altogether more uplifting occasion at Dinamo's stadium but not one that involves football. The success of the Georgian rugby team has allowed sports fans to dream of a different future. Stories of overpaid players are a constant in most countries and Georgia's rugby players offered an antidote. The sport remains amateur in Georgia. When I had met Haig at the Shevardeni Stadium on the way to Rustavi, the likeable Kiwi did not want to leave me waiting outside before we met. 'Come in here while we finish what we're talking about,' said Haig. Incredibly, they went on to pick the starting XV for the Russia game – with a journalist in the room. Players would sleep on gym floors or train in halls with no heating. Many went on to secure contracts abroad, but there seemed to be a collective pursuit of a dream that was absent from Georgian football. That is why there are 52,000 fans at the Boris Paichadze Dinamo Arena. That and the chance to see Russia get hammered.

There was no detachment about the rugby players. Instead, there was a tangible spirit that Georgians connected with, which was typified by the coach, Milton Haig. The likeable Kiwi did not want to leave me waiting outside before we met. 'Come in here while we finish what we're talking about,' said Haig. Incredibly, they were picking the starting XV for the Russia game – with a journalist in the room.

That somehow summed up both Haig as a person but also the Lelos, as the Georgian rugby team were known locally. Many of the players had gone on to play abroad, some, ironically, in the Russian league which, unlike the Georgian competition, was professional. Georgian rugby prospered and, by March 2017, Haig's team had not lost a game in the second-tier European Rugby Championship for six years.

The fans thronged outside the Dinamo stadium, some brandishing the shofar, a traditional Georgian hunting horn, to sound off at the game, others sticking with the cheaper vuvuzela. Neither were present at the football and Dinamo could only have dreamt of the size of the crowd or the enthusiasm generated by the Georgian rugby players. The Georgians liked success and they also liked what the Lelos stood for. 'The footballers have no spirit when they play,' says one passing female Georgian fan, who had transferred her affections to rugby a decade earlier. 'The members of the rugby team are hard-working and with motivation. In every game, you can see that they do everything. I am ashamed when I see our Georgian football team play. It's all about money. They lose their spirit. They don't love football enough. In rugby it's different, they first love what they do and then it's everything else.'

Before the game starts, there is a cacophony as the Russian national anthem is booed. Haig fields many reserve players, who are still so strong that the Russians take 35 minutes to get out of their own half and then only manage that after a Georgian inadvertently fumbles the ball. When a Russian gets into a wrestling match with Mamuka Gorgodze, the home captain and flanker who plays in France for Toulon, the whole crowd are on their feet, heckling and booing. Georgia run out easy winners, 28-14, taking their foot off that gas at the end to allow their Russian opponents a few points and some pride. Thousands flood out of the stadium intoxicated on beer and enthusiasm for a sport on the rise.

Neither the players nor Haig want to run down football, knowing this may alienate their support, but he is still aware of an important shift in Georgian sports culture. 'In terms of people that actually follow the game, it's outgrown football,' he says. 'We are consistently winning and are seeing parents bring children to us rather than football.'

Haig's team had outgrown the European Rugby Championship and needed to take the next step up but, like the Romanians a generation earlier, they were stuck. Georgia had only played the Six Nations whipping-boys Italy once, losing 31-22 in September 2003. In the crossroads of Georgian sport, rugby was being held at a red light, while football looked for new energy in an increasingly unequal landscape. Selling young Georgian players abroad was the only option that might help the national team but it would do little for the club game, particularly if the club scene was dominated by a single rich side.

* * *

I had been fortunate enough to watch football and eat sunflower seeds (or fried bread in Lithuania) in a good few former Soviet states for the BBC World Service and *World Soccer* magazine. The story was usually the same. In the old Soviet league system, one or two clubs from the constituent republics scaled heights that others could not reach. In Cold War times, these were standard-bearers that could match and beat the Russians, like Dynamo Kiev from Ukraine, or Dinamo Tbilisi and Ararat Yerevan from the Caucasus. In a small way, these clubs and their local players made living parallel lives bearable.

When the USSR fell apart, football was ransacked and used for political purposes, or by criminals – or both. Pillaged in one way or another. In Armenia, I had sat in front of Ararat Yerevan's legendary goalkeeper Alyosha Abrahamyan as, stony-faced, he watched the team he once graced play in a stadium so empty that applause was a singular rather than group activity. In 1975, Abrahamyan had kept a clean sheet in front of a 70,000 crowd as then Soviet champions Ararat beat Bayern Munich in the European Cup quarter-finals.

Ararat lost 2-1 on aggregate to the holders and eventual winners but they ran the Germans close.

In Riga, I'd listened to Latvian legend Marian Pahars explain that the old system had some benefits. He was not advocating a return to the USSR, but Pahars's old club Skonto Riga won 14 titles in a row after independence in 1991. Under the control of former KGB officer Guntis Indriksons, who also led the national federation, Skonto monopolised the local league and could compete in European competitions against clubs such as Aberdeen and Chelsea, knocking the former out of the Cup Winners' Cup. Many of those same players took Latvia to the 2004 European Championships, where they deservedly held a poor Germany in Porto, but Skonto are gone and Latvian football is on its knees. 'There is no good or bad,' he said about the old Soviet system, 'but it did work.'

A single dominant and centralised club that is too strong for domestic opposition, but able to compete abroad like BATE in Belarus, Istiqlol in Tajikistan or Altyn Asyr in Turkmenistan gives the impression to outside observers that football in these new republics is strong, but underneath, the game often struggles to survive. Political fudges, corruption, lack of investment and greed mean that only the name links clubs like

Ararat Yerevan or Zalgiris Vilnius in Lithuania with their predecessors on and off the pitch.

The fans have long gone. Many were drawn away by televised games of foreign leagues, particularly the English Premier League, Spain's La Liga and the German Bundesliga. Others trudged away from often-dilapidated stadiums for other sports. The enthusiasm in Georgia for rugby over football was not a one-off. In Riga, the Dinamo ice-hockey club which plays in the pan continental KHL league is the biggest draw. In neighbouring Lithuania, basketball outstrips football, helped by bronze medals at the 1992, 1996 and 2000 Olympic games. Conversely in Azerbaijan, government funding from Europe's version of Qatar is trying to establish football as the most popular sport ahead of chess and wrestling.

Of all these Eastern European experiences, the trip to Tbilisi was the most sobering. Teenage memories came into question that needed grainy YouTube clips for validation. Georgia's footballers had won their independence but had been left behind and that was, perhaps, no surprise. As Nika Jgarkava, the vice-president of the Georgian Football Federation, told me, since independence no one maintained the old communal pitches made available under the Soviet system. Young Georgian players were hoovered up by local clubs, developed and exported like red wine, or almonds, pistachios and walnuts. Local fans were left with their sunflower seeds to support what no one else wanted – or to watch Europe's super clubs on television.

UEFA's response to Eastern European countries that had been so impoverished by the commercialisation of their sport and the looting of loyalties has been to take the Super Cup – the annual showpiece between the winners of the Champions and Europa Leagues – on tour. In 2015, the Super Cup was in Tbilisi. Georgian fans at Dinamo's stadium saw Lionel Messi in the flesh as Barcelona beat Sevilla 5-4. Two years later, the showpiece came to Skopje in what is now North Macedonia, then to the Estonian capital of Tallinn in 2018, but how will these games make fans in these countries watch their own clubs?

How many Georgians among the 52,000 crowd at the Boris Paichadze Dinamo Arena were sufficiently inspired by Messi to subsequently buy a packet of sunflower seeds and then pay two Lari to watch Dinamo? Or even more perversely, after shelling out exorbitant amounts for a Super Cup ticket then go and watch any other team in the Erovnuli Liga for free?

Meanwhile, Milton Haig's Georgian rugby players finally got a game with Italy but on Italian terms. Instead of facing an inevitable Tbilisi wall of sound and the cacophony of the shofar, Georgia played Italy in Florence in November 2018 and lost 28-17.

Between 2017 and the 2019 Rugby World Cup, Georgia only played three matches against tier one sides – one against Argentina and two with Scotland – and only won one of their four matches at the last World Cup. In 2020, Haig stood down and was replaced by local coach Levan Maisashvili. In the wake of the Covid-19 pandemic, an Autumn Nations Cup was staged with the Six Nations teams split into two groups and two guest countries invited. Japan and Fiji were initially chosen. Georgia were ignored. Then in September 2020, Japan dropped out and Georgia were asked as second choice to replace the Brave Blossoms. The celebrations were relatively short-lived as, two days later, Georgian rugby chief Merab Beselia was arrested after shooting an outspoken player, Ramaz Kharazishvili, in the leg, but in November the Lelos got to play a first friendly with England, at Twickenham, albeit admittedly empty due to the pandemic. England beat Georgia 40-0.

At the crossroads of Georgian sport in 2017, football appeared to have stumbled away from its nadir into a new season that avoided the sometimes harsh Georgian winter. In the first season of the Erovnuli Liga played from April to November, Torpedo Kutaisi edged out Dinamo by a point. A year later, Dinamo again finished runners-up, this time trailing Saburtalo before finally winning their first title in four years in 2019, when Lokomotiv also finished in the European places.

In the three seasons since the switch, Georgian clubs have won just one tie in the Champions League, but the Europa League was always a more realistic route, particularly after UEFA introduced a new qualifying path in 2016/17 for domestic title winners dropping out of the Champions League.

The benefits of the switch are starting to show. Torpedo Kutaisi made the play-off round in 2018/19 only to lose 5-4 on aggregate to Bulgarian heavyweights Ludogorets. A year later Dinamo progressed through two rounds before being savaged 5-1 by Feyenoord. But in 2020/21 the club and rivals Lokomotiv were both on the brink of the play-off round. Games were reduced to a single tie due to Covid-19 and a 2-0 defeat in Spain to Granada was no disgrace for Lexo Topuria's Lokomotiv. As title winners, Dinamo were on a different more accessible path. They were drawn against KI from the Faroe Islands, a team from the fishing village of Klavsik, which has a population of just 5,000. KI rely mainly on part-time local players. But Dinamo, the club that had once shocked Liverpool and later won a UEFA trophy, were thrashed, losing by a humiliating 6-1.

Georgia is a fine country, fantastic people, food and wine, and, like the Lelos, the national football team is competitive. They reached the much-delayed play-off for Euro 2020 but narrowly lost out to North Macedonia. Yet those footballers play mostly abroad. No club from Georgia will ever win a European trophy again. The remaining fans left watching local matches have just sunflower seeds and the memories captured in curling old photos for sustenance.

Pay No Attention to That Man Behind the Curtain

by James Montague

DPRK v Lebanon
Asian Cup qualifier
Pyongyang, North Korea
5 September 2017

The gate for Air Koryo flight JS152 to Pyongyang can be found in the farthest corner of the Beijing Capital International Airport. On any given week there are only a handful of flights leaving for the Democratic People's Republic of Korea, but today the flight is full. Among the well-connected Koreans returning home, wearing red pin badges of the Great Leader Kim Il-sung or his son, the Dear Leader Kim Jong-il, proudly on their breasts, the Lebanon national team is not difficult to miss. The players are wearing red training tops with 'LEBANON' stitched on to the back in huge letters. The hall is subdued, as if the squad of perhaps 30 players and officials nervously await bad news.

We were headed to Pyongyang for a 2019 AFC Asian Cup qualification match. It was a rare home fixture for North Korea, who had not played one in Pyongyang for almost two years. They had been drawn in the same group as Lebanon, Hong Kong and Malaysia, and the federation decided to hire a foreign coach, only the second time they had ever done that. His name was Jørn Andersen, a former Norway international striker who in 1990 became the first foreigner to be the top scorer in Germany's Bundesliga. Real-world events, however, had stymied Andersen's campaign.

The first thing was the assassination. Both games against Malaysia had been postponed when the half-brother of North Korea's young leader Kim Jong-un was murdered in a bizarre plot using a nerve agent at Kuala Lumpur airport. No one knew when the matches would be played. Or even if they ever could be played. And then there were the nuclear bombs. Since Kim Jong-un came to power in 2011, North Korea had accelerated its weapons programme. In just six years Kim Jong-un had ordered three nuclear tests, each exponentially more powerful than the previous. A few days before the Lebanese team and I had arrived at the Beijing Capital International Airport, the North Korean military fired an intercontinental ballistic missile over Japan, suggesting it now had the technical capabilities to hit US territory as well as America's Asian allies.

As we milled around the gate, waiting to board, it was clear the players were on edge. 'Everyone is worried back home,' says Omar Bugiel in an English accent. Omar is a 23-year-old striker with Forest Green Rovers hoping to make his Lebanese debut against North Korea. Everyone on the team comes from divergent corners of the earth, the product of a civil war in the 1980s that spread its sons and daughters far and wide. Lebanon's population is around six million. Perhaps as much as four times that number live around the world. Bugiel's family had found refuge from the civil war in Germany, where he was born, before he came to the UK as a teenager.

Soony Saad, sitting nearby, briefly considered not coming at all. 'At first I thought, maybe I should say I'm injured,' he says half-jokingly. 'You see the news and all this nuclear war stuff.' Soony was born in the US, in Dearborn, Michigan, where a third of the city identify as Arab Americans. He played as a striker for the US under-17 and under-20 teams but switched to the country of his father's birth when the opportunities in American soccer dried up. Now he was travelling to North Korea at a time when the few American citizens left in the country had gone the other way.

Twenty-four hours earlier the US government had placed a ban on any US citizen from entering North Korea. It was retaliation for the death of Otto Warmbier, a 19-year-old student who was arrested while on holiday in North Korea for trying to steal a propaganda poster off the wall of his hotel. He was eventually sentenced to 15 years' hard labour. No one knows exactly what happened to Warmbier but when he was released a few months ago he was in a coma and had been for a while. He died six days after returning to the US. 'I thought about it and realised this happens once in your life, going to see North Korea,' says Soony. 'But I told the team manager: get my American passport as far from the Koreans as possible whilst I'm there.'

Pyongyang is only a 90-minute flight. Air Koryo stewardesses, their faces white with make-up, hurry up and down the aisle before the plane lands at the newly built Pyongyang International Airport, which opened in 2016. We appear to be the first and only plane of the day. Military aircraft and long-mothballed civilian jets in various states of decay line the runway. It seems empty. A sign, rather hopefully, points the way for transit passengers.

Once through passport control and after picking up our bags, a line of soldiers search our possessions, looking for books or USBs – anything that might bring prohibited reading material or films into the country. The players check their phones in vain for a wi-fi signal. 'Is there any internet?' Omar asks hopefully. There isn't but, with the right permissions and forms, it was possible for foreign visitors to buy a 3G SIM card with a tiny amount of data for $250. This doesn't seem to impress anyone. For the next few days, at least, Omar, Soony and the rest of the Lebanese national team would be cut off from the outside world.

* * *

There are a series of strict rules to be followed when you arrive to meet the Eternal Leaders of Juche Korea, but one must be adhered to above all the others. In a large, sparse, darkened room, deep inside the Kumsusan Palace of the Sun in Pyongyang, Kim Il-sung is lying on a deep red velvet pile in a glass sarcophagus. His embalmed body is lit from underneath. In the gloom, at the edges of the room, soldiers watch as you approach to make sure you pay your respects correctly. I had been briefed by my guide that I *must* bow deeply three times, first at his feet, then at either side. But never at the head, which is seen as highly offensive in Korean culture. I comply.

Next door, a trophy room of sorts is festooned with the gifts and honours bestowed on the Great Leader. Framed photos show Kim Il-sung warmly embracing a slew of iconic Communists, Josip Broz Tito, Fidel Castro and Mao Zedong among them. The cabinets heave with trophies and medals and certificates. There is even a 1993 presidential medal from the inauguration of one William Jefferson Clinton, back when negotiations between the US and North Korea might still have avoided a nuclear Korean peninsula.

Kim Il-sung was the founding father of North Korea. He cut his teeth as a guerrilla leader in China, fighting against Japanese imperialism. After the Second World War, with Korea deeply divided and with backing from the Soviet Union, he founded the Democratic People's Republic of Korea north of the 36th parallel, an attempt to create a communist utopia that was heavily dependent on Chinese and Soviet subsidies. In 1950, the north invaded the US-backed south. The resulting Korea War – fought against a US-led UN force – took four million lives. Pyongyang was virtually destroyed. When the fighting ceased in 1953 both sets of troops were back to where they had started. There has never been a peace treaty. The two sides are still, to this day, technically at war. The 250km-long Demilitarized Zone, the DMZ, separates them.

In North Korea they see the war differently. At the Fatherland Liberation War Museum, guests are invited to watch a film called *Why America Started the War*. It is the only time the word America is used. From then on, the US is referred to by florid, disparaging euphemism; the 'arrogant aggressors', the 'foolhardy imperialist' or, simply, as 'the incompetents'. Still, life was better for Koreans in the north rather than the south during much of the 20th century, even as Kim Il-sung built a brutal state apparatus around his cult of personality, and around the quasi-religious state ideology of Juche, an ultra-nationalist philosophy that places self-reliance above all else.

Today, North Korea is one of the most repressive regimes in the world. Every year it is bottom of Reporters Without Borders Press Freedom Index. It is 172 out of 174 on Transparency International's Corruption Perceptions Index. North Korea is a brutal one-party communist dictatorship where zero dissent is tolerated. Defectors relay stories of the public execution of party elites, generals and other power rivals who have been purged in the most gruesome manner: sometimes by being tied to the muzzle of an anti-aircraft battery and reduced to a red mist. Human rights groups have interviewed defectors who have told stories of vast concentration camps for political crimes as well as arbitrary torture and human experimentation. And it wasn't just the dissenters imprisoned, but the families of dissenters including their children. And not just their children, but their children's children. Punishment in North Korea is hereditary. 'North Korea is a country where life is nasty brutish and short for a lot of people,' said Christopher Green, an academic at Leiden University in the Netherlands who specialises in North Korean sport and has interviewed hundreds of defectors. 'Life is unforgiving.'

Kim Il-sung died in 1994 with his country in a deep economic crisis. The collapse of the Soviet Union cut off North Korea's main source of trade. A succession of droughts led to a crippling famine where as many as 2.5 million people perished. Next door in the Kumsusan Palace of the Sun lies his son and heir Kim Jong-il. Unlike his father, his trophy room is noticeably absent of international recognition, reflecting the country's political and economic isolation from the 1990s onwards. The only recognisable statesmen who sent tributes seem to be Robert Mugabe of Zimbabwe and Ali Bongo Ondimba of Gabon. Under Kim Jong-il, North Korea's thirst for nuclear weapons increased, but the Dear Leader also began to recognise they had a competitive advantage in sport. 'North Korea needs to show to the domestic audience they have strength and the ability to succeed,' says Christopher Green. 'Sport is one way of doing that. They take it seriously.'

Investment was made in the men's and women's game. There were attempts to create a united Korean football team (a united team played at the 1991 FIFA Youth World Championship). Basketball was promoted as a way of building a strength after the crippling famine. FIFA began to bring the north in from the cold. So much so that former FIFA president Sepp Blatter visited in 2002. 'It felt like I was travelling back in time, flying two hours by plane, and travelling back 50 years,' said Jerome Champagne, a former FIFA presidential candidate who was Blatter's political advisor and helped arrange the trip.

South Korea was about to co-host the 2002 World Cup finals with Japan and some in FIFA were worried at how the north would react. South Korean intelligence believed that Kim Jong-il was the guiding hand behind the Korea Air 858 bombing in 1987 which killed all 115 people on board and was seen as an attempt to disrupt the summer Olympics taking place in South Korea's capital Seoul the following year. 'One of the lines was that we had to help DPRK football,' said Champagne. 'But the more we were engaged in helping North Korea football the less tempted the regime would be to disrupt the World Cup in 2002.' Blatter didn't meet the Dear Leader but he did meet the head of state and promised funding for new all-weather pitches and help organising training camps in Switzerland. The 2002 finals passed without incident.

Over the years I've watched football matches in some of the hardest to reach places: Gaza, Yemen, Iraq during the height of its civil war. But every attempt to watch a match in North Korea had ended in failure. I first saw the North Korean men's team in the flesh in 2004. I had just moved to Dubai, in the United Arab Emirates, and came across a story in a local paper about a 2006 World Cup qualifier taking place against the UAE in Dubai that evening. It was a dead rubber, but it was taking place next to my apartment.

It was a surreal experience. Usually, you would be lucky to find 20 people in the crowd for a game like that. But, on a hot, humid evening, dozens of coaches with bars on their windows had arrived at the Al Rashid Stadium. Nearly 2,000 North Korean fans had been brought to the game. The women wore colourful, traditional dress, carrying thick, rectangular pieces of wood, tied to their hands with orange thread, to aid their clapping; the men wore identical, dark work suits with red Kim Jong-il pin badges. They filled a whole stand, segregated by sex. A ring of North Korean security men surrounded the stand. Rather than face the pitch, they faced the crowd. The North Korean fans haunting chants seesawed throughout the game. After the final whistle, the supporters all marched silently back on to their allotted coaches. Later I would discover they were labourers and maids living in the UAE, sent out of the country to earn foreign currency.

North Korea has been under intense economic sanctions for decades and the government would take as much as two thirds of their wages to try and fill the gap. But the game sparked more questions. Who were the players? What teams did they play for in North Korea? According to the team sheet I had managed to nab at the Al-Rashid Stadium the dominant domestic team appeared to be called 4.25. What did that name mean? And what did the league even look like? Could they watch European football back home? Would they know who Messi or Ronaldo were?

For the next few years I tried in vain to travel to North Korea and find out what football in the country actually looked like. But the DPR Korea Football Association was notoriously hard to contact. Even FIFA had trouble contacting them. 'We would send a fax,' says Jerome Champagne. 'Sometimes we'd hear back.' Today, there is a single Hotmail address. Over the best part of a decade I've periodically tried it, and never had a reply.

Even after North Korea qualified for the 2010 World Cup finals, their first since 1966, it was impossible to get in. I tried to go undercover to play in an amateur golf tournament that was being held in Pyongyang. I'd found a British golf club who would vouch (rather erroneously) that I was in fact a scratch golfer. But the organisers were wise to that. Instead, I travelled to Switzerland where the national team regularly held training camps. On a pitch high up in the Alps, I finally met a North Korean international. Jong Tae-se was the team's star striker and a member of the *Zainichi*: Japanese-born Koreans. He'd been dubbed 'The People's Rooney' by an English tabloid for his likeness to England's record goalscorer, although I couldn't see the resemblance at all. 'Everyone keeps saying this about Rooney!' he said, laughing, when I got to speak to him pitch side for CNN, green hills and snow-capped Swiss mountains surrounding us. 'I don't want to be like Rooney, I want to play like Didier Drogba.'

For two days I followed the squad as they travelled to Austria, to play Greece in a warm-up game. The squad was friendly but standoffish and then all contact was broken, when two days before the game, North Korea sunk a South Korean warship, the *Cheonan*, killing 46 sailors. The North Korean FA considered

CNN to be the same as the CIA and so I was now *persona non grata*. The match still went ahead, though, ending in a creditable 2-2 draw.

The North Koreans would prove just as mysterious in South Africa. After a spirited performance against Brazil where they narrowly lost 2-1, they ended up being hammered 7-0 by Portugal. Stories began appearing in the foreign media that the coach and players were severely punished when they returned home. Hard labour was mentioned, although a FIFA investigation later concluded there was no evidence for the claim. Eighteen months after the 2010 World Cup finals, Kim Jong-il died, his body was embalmed, and he was interned into the Kumsusan Palace of the Sun next to his father.

His youngest son Kim Jong-un would surprisingly emerge as his successor. And for a few years it seemed that relations between North Korea and the outside world were thawing. In 2012 the Associated Press was allowed to open a bureau in the country, the first Western news organisation to do so. The new leader talked about opening the economy and mirroring China's phenomenal growth. So, at the beginning of 2017, I started e-mailing the Hotmail address of the DPRK's FA again. Still there was no reply but I did get a positive response from Koryo Tours, a British-run travel agency based in Beijing who specialised in trips to North Korea. One of the company's owners had been a producer on *The Game of Their Lives*, a BBC documentary about North Korea's 1966 World Cup team. They could get me in to see an Asian Cup qualifier against Malaysia. It was impossible to be accredited as a journalist. But I would be allowed in to cover it under the assumption that I was. That was good enough for me.

Alas, that game never happened. Kim Jong-un's half-brother – Kim Jong-nam – was murdered at Kuala Lumpur airport. Two women had approached him as he came off a flight and smeared him with an unknown substance. It was later determined that the two substances reacted to create VX, a nerve agent, which quickly killed him. The two women, one from Vietnam and the other from Indonesia, were arrested but both had a strange but highly credible story. Both said they had been hired by men claiming to be TV producers. They thought they were part of a Candid Camera-type prank show. It was widely believed that Kim Jong-un ordered his brother's death. Malaysia was furious that such a dangerous operation was conducted on its soil. North Korea's ambassador was expelled, and Malaysian citizens were prevented from leaving Pyongyang, effectively being held hostage.

Unsurprisingly the match between North Korea and Malaysia was postponed.

As the months passed the tension rose. Donald Trump was elected US president which initially made the situation worse. But, incredibly, it was still planned that the Lebanon game in September go ahead. I booked my flight to Beijing and waited for my visa, locking my press card in the safe at Koryo Tour's HQ. It wasn't until I saw the Lebanese players at the Beijing Capital International Airport that I truly believed it was going to happen. But, once inside, I had a schedule to keep.

Technically I was a tourist so I was taken from monument to statue to museum by two kind female guides and my driver, who I suspected was a spy as he couldn't actually drive. The schedule took us to the Kumsusan Palace of the Sun and the embalmed bodies of the Eternal Leader and his son. Afterwards I was handed back my camera and my phone.

The sun was shining as hundreds of smartly dressed Koreans arrived on coaches for their tour. For a brief moment, by the well-kept gardens and ponds by the entrance, it felt idyllic. I turned on my phone and received a push alert from the *New York Times*. At midday, 600km north-east of Pyongyang, and at almost the exact time I had been standing in front of the embalmed body of Kim Il-sung, a huge explosion was felt at the Punggye-ri military testing site, a network of tunnels below Mount Mantap. The explosion measured 6.3 on the Richter scale, but it wasn't an earthquake. North Korea had just detonated a nuclear bomb.

* * *

Omar Bugiel and Soony Saad are sitting in their room high up in the Koryo Hotel playing their PlayStation 4, and trying to take their minds off the possibility of nuclear Armageddon. 'Thank God this works,' Omar says, pointing to the console. The two are playing *FIFA 2018*, Liverpool versus Manchester United. 'We still don't have any internet,' says Omar as Soony directs Sadio Mane to score the opening goal. 'And no way of contacting home to tell them we are okay.' It was Soony who first realised something big had happened. No one felt the explosion, of course, but Soony had seen an impromptu celebration. 'I woke up and there was this sound of thousands of people chanting something nearby, as if they were going to a game,' Soony recalls. 'Then I turned on the TV and there's one channel, RT [Russia Today]. I saw that North Korea had tested a hydrogen bomb. I didn't know if it was the start of a war.'

None of us did. Since the explosion the Lebanese team had been shuttled between their hotel and the Kim Il-sung Stadium for training unsure whether this was, in fact, the end of the world. News was hard to come by and I was worried that, as a journalist who wasn't officially there as a journalist, I might be arrested or held hostage. I had assumed that my hotel room was being bugged and all my conversations recorded. So did the players. What they had seen of the city had been through the curtains of the team bus; of clean, largely empty streets; of soldiers and huge golden statues built in honour of the Eternal Leaders of Juche Korea; of a mysterious pyramid-shaped building outside of their hotel window. The briefest snapshot of a country and its people. Everything seemed calm. 'The statues are crazy,' says Omar. 'It's like travelling to Germany in World War Two or communist Soviet Union. Statues and portraits everywhere. We trained at the Kim Il-sung Stadium and it had two huge portraits of Kim's family outside.'

Soony's American passport wasn't far from his mind. He was born and raised in the US, playing soccer in, as he puts it, 'the hot house local leagues' in Michigan where immigrant teams would play each other, and often fight. 'It isn't just Arabs there [in Dearborn],' Soony explains. 'There's Poles, Serbs, Albanians. It's a deep soccer culture. I would go back in the winter and play the local tournaments. It would be crazy. You'd get players turning up with baseball bats.'

At one point it seemed Soony was destined for the senior US men's national team. He was part of the United States Soccer Federation's programme at the IMG Academy in Bradenton, Florida, where the country's best talents are nurtured, but he always felt like an outsider. 'Bradenton wasn't ready for a Muslim American,' he says. 'There was no mosque. I would bring my own halal meat. Dad would prepare chicken breasts and freeze them for me to take!' After playing for the under-20 team, his international career stalled, until one day he got a call from Theo Bucker, a German coach who had come close in 2014 to taking Lebanon to their first World Cup finals. 'I scored on my debut!' Soony says proudly.

After a spell in the Thai league he moved back to the US and now played for Sporting Kansas City in Major League Soccer, featuring regularly for Lebanon. He wondered what would happen if he scored in the Kim Il-sung Stadium. 'It is in the back of your mind,' he admits. 'What if I score and they find out I am an American?' His parents had tried to talk him out of going. 'They said, "Are you sure? Is it worth taking the risk just for a game?"' Soony says. 'But when else are you going to see this? We are treating it professionally. We need the points. Although we don't know any of their players. There were some YouTube videos but we don't have any of them as the internet doesn't work so I'm a bit in the dark.' The North Korean team on *FIFA 18* hadn't given any insight into their opponents either. 'It's not really accurate,' says Soony. 'Omar is on it!' Omar shifts awkwardly in his seat. 'Yeah,' he replies, unhappily. EA Sports, the developer of *FIFA 18*, had given him a rating of 54. When the ratings were announced he tweeted the game's publisher to complain, '@easportsfifa 54?? Basically saying Ive got two left feet & tackle my own players.'

'I should be 75 to 80,' he adds. 'He should!' Soony shouts encouragingly.

Omar's journey had been equally as circuitous as Soony's. After leaving Germany for the UK he eventually found his way into non-league football. At the beginning of the year he signed for Forest Green Rovers and, a few months later, the team secured promotion to League Two after beating Tranmere Rovers 3-1 in the National League play-off final at Wembley. 'After the Wembley game, I got the call out of the blue from Lebanon. It was an amazing month!' says Omar, who is constantly asking questions about North Korea and things he has seen. He was hoping to make his debut against North Korea but, aside from the prospect of war, he had enjoyed the experience and the unexpected break from the internet. 'It's helped us bond,' he says. After a few hours of internet withdrawal, the players would now get together and tell each other about their lives. 'No one is on their phone so everyone has been talking to each other,' he says. 'Things I wouldn't have known about because we've actually talked to each other.'

Their game of *FIFA* is interrupted by chanting, coming from outside. Soony and Omar rush to the window to see what is going on. On a rooftop, next door, several dozen men dressed in identical work clothes are marching and waving large flags in a choreographed display.

'What *is* that huge building in the distance, like a rocket?' Soony says pointing to the pyramid-like building in the near distance.

It is the unfinished Ryugyong Hotel, I tell him.

'What, all of it?' Omar adds, incredulously. 'Is it true that people who live in Pyongyang are chosen people?' he asks. Someone had told him that only the best connected, who have proven their absolute loyalty to the Kim family, can live in the capital. 'This place,' Soony says as we all look out of the window, unsure of what purpose the display serves, 'is crazy.'

* * *

Pyongyang didn't fear an impending nuclear war, largely because they didn't know anything about it. It took a few days for the news to be reported, although there had been some warning signs. On the morning of the test, *Rodong Sinmun*, the Workers' newspaper and the state organ of choice to convey official news to the people, published a full-colour front-page photo of Kim Jong-un standing next to a hydrogen bomb. 'He watched an H-bomb to be loaded into new ICBM,' read the story. 'Saying that he felt the pride of indomitably bolstering up the nuclear forces at a great price while seeing the Juche-oriented thermonuclear weapon with super explosive power made by our own efforts and technology.'

The city is sweltering under an early autumn heatwave but, unlike other Asian metropoles like Beijing or Bangkok, Pyongyang is not a broiling jumble of traffic and commerce, neon and smog. The city is quiet and clean, with wide streets that see only intermittent traffic. Kim Il-sung Square, with its long dais filled with military officials and occasionally Kim Jong-un when massive parades pass by, is empty and silent. Tributes and posters and statues to the Kim family, which has ruled North Korea for nearly seven decades, can be found everywhere. The largest tribute is a 22m-high bronze statue of Kim Il-sung on Mansudae Hill. His son was cast and added next to him after he died.

As one of the last communist dictatorships, adverts are banned but every street corner has colourful hand-painted propaganda billboards extolling the country's nuclear missile programme while denouncing US imperialist aggression. My guides direct me to where I am allowed to walk. Most shops are off-limits, as is paying for anything in the local currency, the won (although there is a Chinese-owned mall where foreigners are allowed to visit, and you pay in local money). There's a trip to Pyongyang's small metro line with East German-made trains. People crowd around the display copies of that day's *Rodong Sinmun*. On the trains, which fill to bursting with commuters, televisions have been installed. Today's film is a dramatisation of North Korea's women's team winning the 2006 FIFA Under-20 World Cup.

In fact, it is women's football that is the dominant game in North Korea largely because women's football has been far more successful in recent years. They have won three AFC Asian Cups, gold medals at three Asian Games and – at the time – are under-17 and under-20 world champions. A few weeks later they would win the AFC Under-16 Women's Championship by beating

South Korea in the final. The senior women's team has qualified for twice as many World Cups as the men, although there was scandal after their last appearance, at the 2011 finals in Germany. Five players failed a drugs test. The North Korean delegation claimed they had accidentally failed the test due to taking a traditional Chinese medicine extracted from a deer's musk gland. The medicine was administered, the delegation claimed, after several players were hit by a lightning strike while training. FIFA didn't buy it, and North Korea was banned from the 2015 World Cup.

On a large island in the slow-moving Taedong River, which cuts through Pyongyang, a women's league match is taking place at the May Day Stadium. The stadium is by some counts the largest in the world. Until a recent renovation, 150,000 people would come here to see the Mass Games, a huge, choreographed event that would feature thousands of gymnasts. You can see the vast May Day Stadium as you cross the Taedong; a massive concrete blancmange that looks as if a steampunk spaceship has crash-landed on top of a football pitch. Inside, the terraces rise steeply. When full, it must be an incredible sight. But it is not full today.

All football teams in North Korea are attached to different industries, factories or government departments, be they cigarette companies, the navy or the dockyards. Unsurprisingly given that North Korea has an estimated one million-strong standing army and a highly militarised public space, the army has dominated North Korean football. The most successful side has been 4.25, which – I finally discovered – is named after 25 April, the day the North Korean army was founded. But league matches are a mystery. Fixtures are not published. Games are announced outside the stadium the day before. And, besides, for many years there has not been a league in the traditional sense. Instead both the men's and women's domestic game is a series of knockout tournaments, held every two months all year round, usually taking place around big public holidays, like Kim Il-sung's birthday or Army Day. The teams are then ranked according to their performance over the six tournaments.

Today, Sobaeksu, a subsidiary team of 4.25, is playing Amrokkang Sports Club, the team of internal security, in a match featuring four players who have been capped by the full women's national team. The vast stadium of close to 120,000 seats is almost empty. A few hundred supporters have turned up, mainly the players from their corresponding men's team. Their chants echo around the vast stadium, 'Cheer up, cheer up, Amrokkang!'

The cheering stops the moment I turn and try to take a picture. Sobaeksu score three goals without reply, including a stunning free kick that no goalkeeper could have stopped. There were no team sheets. The goalscorer's name remains a mystery.

Even though North Korea remains a deeply patriarchal society, the women's team is a source of huge pride. When Kim Jong-un came to power, one of his first policies was to instruct greater investment in sport and especially football as it built international prestige and brought vital foreign currency into the country. At the only English language book shop in Pyongyang, which is full of translated copies of speeches and books glorifying the Kim family's every utterance, I found one that Kim Jong-un had written about sport, entitled *Let Us Usher In a New Golden Age of Building a Sports Power in the Revolutionary Spirit of Paektu*. (Paektu is a mountain in the north, next to the Chinese border, that became the stronghold for Kim Il-sung's guerrilla army and is now mythologised. The North claims Kim Jong-il was born here although historians have questioned that.) It was a letter sent out to the attendees of the Seventh National Conference of Sportspeople on 25 March 2015. Or the year Juche 104. In North Korea they count the years from the date of Kim Il-sung's birth.

The letter lays out how important sport is to Kim Jong-un and his government. And why. In it he writes, 'Sports play a very important role in consolidating a nation's strength, adding lustre to a country's prestige and honour, inspiring people with national pride and dignity and imbuing the whole society with revolutionary mettle.'

More importantly, sport in general and football in particular was an ongoing part of the Fatherland Liberation War, and the goal of unifying the Korean peninsula, 'Sportspeople should regard their training programmes as combat orders given by the party and their training arena as a battlefield for implementing the Party's ideas and defending their country.'

The first sport that North Korea should seek global supremacy in, according to Kim Jong-un, is women's football. 'Kim Jong-un comes to power in 2012 and suddenly the physical education curriculum focused much more on football,' explained Christopher Green. 'Classrooms in high school are suddenly reorganised into football teams for training. A defector told me, "It didn't matter if they liked football or not. Kim Jung-un liked football."' A country-wide talent search was started, and the newly discovered players would be sent to a new football academy, the Pyongyang International Football School, and then into the various national teams before potentially being sent abroad.

A short drive away from the May Day Stadium, at the Kang Ban-sok Middle School, Kim Jong-un's plan is being put into action.

A large, sand-based football pitch is filled with hundreds of teenagers. One large group in school uniform is dancing together in large circles. A few hundred are dressed in brown uniforms with berets; army cadets marching in formation. The louche musicians who make up the school's brass band are sitting on the school steps waiting for practice. In one corner, Chong Yong-jin is trying to improve his team's shooting accuracy. The 57-year-old coach of the school team, dressed in a bright-yellow goalkeeper's jersey and trucker cap with a whistle around his neck, has lined up his mixed group of boys and girls. Each takes it in turn to dribble and then shoot at a green painted wall, divided into different sections, with points awarded for hitting the corners. Each player takes it in turn to drill the ball into the corner as the army cadets march and sing patriotic songs around them.

The girls are far more accurate than the wayward boys. 'I've been teaching for five years and the girls are better than the boys,' Chong agrees when he takes a break. 'They have won medals. They have won finals.'

Since 2012 the boys and girls have played together, Chong says, to help the boys improve. 'Now that the female team is more popular,' he adds, 'we are putting more effort into the boys' team.'

There are no Barcelona or Manchester United or AC Milan tops. A few players wear the jerseys of local teams, but more wear the red shirt of the national team. Chong is a fan of 4.25, as almost everyone who I ask is. 'But I like them all equally,' he quickly adds. He still plays himself ('I am a goalkeeper and 80 per cent of the match is down to the goalkeeper,' he tells me.) and is as vague on what the league system here looks like as everyone else is. 'There are two groups, A and B,' he says eventually. 'They play each other, the winner, for the championship, five or six times a year.'

The sun is draining from the sky and the crowds of children begin to filter away, including his players. But they will all be there again tomorrow afternoon, and the afternoon after that. 'I have hope that we will see these players trying out for the national team,' he says. 'My greatest success is to come!'

* * *

In the foyer of the Pyongyang International Football School hangs a huge, framed photo, almost four feet wide and two feet tall, behind a velvet rope and illuminated by spotlight. It shows Kim Jong-un shaking hands with members of the North Korean men's national team. Some of the players are visibly emotional as Kim leans over to shake their hands after a game at the Kim Il-sung Stadium. The school was set up on Kim Jong-un's instruction in 2013. He visited the school shortly afterwards and a message he wrote is inscribed into stone near the entrance.

The school is a short walk from the May Day Stadium, on Rungrado Island. There are 20 all-weather football pitches here. On the smaller pitches, groups of teenagers in red national team jerseys are playing a game of one-touch football. In the centre, in short sleeves and slacks with a red Kim Il-sung pin badge, Kim Chol-ung isn't happy. He blows his whistle to stop the game and marches on to the pitch, telling the players where they have gone wrong before blasting his whistle to start the action again. He stops it a few seconds later and repeats his instructions.

'The first step is in the ordinary schools, that is the regional school you saw,' says Kim, who is the deputy director of the school, once he is happy enough to let the play continue. 'Each province has 50 schools. And those 50 schools have their own football teams. We go to the provinces, find the players and they come here.' Kim, who is in his 50s and played for the electric tram

Fans of Iran celebrate their 2-1 victory against the USA at the 1998 World Cup finals in Lyon, France. Several can be seen wearing T-shirts bearing the image of Maryam Rajavi, leader of the People's Mujahedin of Iran. June 1998.

A supporter of Feyenoord holds up a photo of recently murdered Dutch politician Pim Fortuyn before their UEFA Cup Final match against Borussia Dortmund in Rotterdam. May 2002.

Carlos Tevez shortly after his team Corinthians are beaten by River Plate in the Copa Libertadores in São Paulo, Brazil. The 3-1 defeat sparked riots in the ground and, later, across the city. May 2006.

Arsenal's Rachel Yankey shrugs off her opponent during the 2007 Women's UEFA Cup Final against Umeå of Sweden. The game finished 0-0, and Arsenal were crowned champions of Europe. April 2007.

Palestinian supporters standing in front of a Yasser Arafat billboard at the Faisal Al-Husseini Stadium in Al-Ram for first-ever, near Ramallah. The match, a 2012 Olympic Games qualifier against Thailand, was Palestine's first-ever competitive match on home soil. March 2011.

The national anthems are played before Palestine v Thailand in a 2012 Olympic Games qualifier in Al-Ram, near Ramallah. The three dignitaries are Salam Fayyad, former Palestinian prime minister, Mohamed bin Hammam, the former president of the AFC, and Jibril Rajoub, president of the Palestinian Football Association. March 2011.

Supporters of Beitar Jerusalem before a game at the Teddy Stadium in Jerusalem. March 2012.

A collage of black and white newspaper cuttings, in Georgian, of Dinamo Tbilisi's winning of the 1981 UEFA Cup campaign, hanging in the club house of FC Rustavi. March 2017.

Merab Shonia from the Georgian rugby supporters' club blows a shofar, made from a ram's horn, at a rugby union international.

Shooting practice at the Kang Ban-sok Middle School in Pyongyang. The teams are mixed due to the girls being much more advanced than the boys. September 2017.

Pupils at the Pyongyang International Football School lining up before their first practice session of the day. September 2017.

Players, staff and supporters celebrate on stage in Reykjavík's main square after beating Kosovo and qualifying for the 2018 World Cup. The victory meant that Iceland became the smallest country to ever qualify for the finals. October 2017.

Tens of thousands of Boca Juniors supporters turn up at La Bombonera stadium to watch their team train before the Copa Libertadores Final against hated rivals River Plate. November 2018.

A Cameroon supporter flies his country's flag during a Women's World Cup last-16 match between England and Cameroon. June 2019.

company's team for 15 years, proudly shows me around the school. There are 500 children here, he says, from the age of seven to 16. We pass classrooms as children are being taught geometry and geography. A library is full of football books and periodicals in Korean. Football theory is taught in a lecture hall nearby.

Kim fell in love with the game at 13, when he heard the exploits of the 1966 World Cup team – who famously beat Italy and almost knocked out Portugal in the quarter-finals – on the radio. Now he's one of the men in charge of nurturing the next generation of senior men's and women's internationals. 'In May 2013, that was when we started to develop our sports, especially football, to bring a high level like the other countries so we established this academy,' he says. 'Thanks to this academy a lot of future players are educated and grown here.' The failure to get to Russia 2018 was, of course, a setback. But the first graduates will fall out next year. Already '80 per cent of the players from the under-16 and 17 team' come from the academy. The aim is Qatar 2022. 'All these players are going there,' he says without doubt.

Kim Chol-ung is about to wrap up for the day. Later this afternoon his students will be at the Kim Il-sung Stadium, working as ball boys during the North Korea v Lebanon match. The game will not be shown live on TV. They never are, not since the authorities decided to show the North Korea-Portugal game from the 2010 World Cup finals – which Portugal won 7-0. But football matches from European leagues are regularly shown on TV, Kim says, usually long after they've been played. Recently he has seen PSG and Manchester United play. And although he respects Messi and Ronaldo's talents, the best team he has seen recently is Bayern Munich.

'Who is your favourite player,' I ask.

'Thomas Muller,' he replies. He taps a finger against his temple.

'He thinks,' says Kim. 'Thinking, decision-making, striking.'

* * *

Thousands of men and women march past the Arch of Triumph, up a wide boulevard and towards the Kim Il-sung Stadium. They are quiet, a low hum following them as they walk, and dressed in near identical clothing. Entry for the match is free, and most of the seats are taken up with schoolboys and schoolgirls wearing white shirts, black trousers or skirts, a red tie and the ubiquitous pin badge. Despite the nuclear bomb and the related political fall-out (most of which we don't yet know about), the game between North Korea and Lebanon is still on. There are no shirts or scarves to be bought. In fact, the women selling the daily sports newspaper from a small table by the entrance refused to sell me a copy because I was a foreigner.

Inside, the stadium is almost full, but not with the 100,000 supporters that the state media has reported are in attendance. The stadium holds, at most, 40,000 people. But once inside the chants begin. A long speech is read out on behalf of the Minister for Physical Culture and Sports before the teams come out and the national anthems are played.

Both Omar and Soony have to make do with a seat on the bench. This will be the first home game for Jørn Andersen, the coach of the North Korea team, but he can call on a lot of experience, and a surprising number of players who have played abroad. His goalkeeper is Ri Myong-guk, who played all three games at the 2010 World Cup finals, including the 7-0 defeat to Portugal. Also from that World Cup team is midfielder Pak Song-chol. Three of his squad are Japanese-born Koreans, although Jon Tae-se has long departed the team. Two others briefly played in the Serbian third tier, while midfielder Jong Il-gwan currently plays for Luzern in Switzerland. Young striker Pak Kwang-ryong plays for SKN St. Pölten in the Austrian top division after playing in

Switzerland for six years. But Han Kwang-song, who plays for Perugia and became the first North Korean player to score in Serie A, is not in the squad. No one knows why.

Andersen is so animated as he gives his instructions that, from a distance, it looks like his blond curtains are flapping up and down. But North Korea are in control. After a good start the Lebanon players seem to be struggling with the Kim Il-sung Stadium's artificial pitch. The noise from the crowd is high-pitched and piercing when North Korea take the lead through striker Kim Yu-song's looping header. But in the first few minutes of the second half, Lebanon level after defender Nour Mansour ghosts in at the back post and blasts the ball in.

It was, unexpectedly, a high-quality game. But Lebanon needed to make some early changes because of injury. I thought of Omar and Soony and how they were now unlikely to play, after everything that had happened. Andersen also had some problems and had used all his substitutes by the 60th minute. Although they seemed to quickly pay off. With just a few minutes left, one of North Korea's Japan-born players – Ri Yong-jik – fired in from outside the box during a defensive mix-up. There are few chances for catharsis in North Korean society, but the resulting noise felt like an earthquake. Or an underground nuclear explosion. The ground shook as the players returned to their positions.

There was just a few minutes left and Lebanon's Montenegrin coach Miodrag Radulović finally brought on Soony as his third substitute and his last roll of the dice. Omar would have to wait another day to make his debut. Soony darted around the North Korean penalty box as the Lebanon team pushed for an unlikely equaliser. The crowd willed North Korea on. Everyone had a part to play, including the ball boys from the Pyongyang International Football School. With the match deep in injury time, and the ball out of play near North Korea's penalty area, one of the Lebanese players on the bench, Maher Sabra, decided that one ball boy was deliberately returning the ball too slowly. A tussle took place on the touchline. When Sabra wrestled the ball out of the teenage Korean's hands, he blasted it back at him, narrowly missing his head. The crowd started screaming at the pitch. Objects were thrown. The situation was about to boil over and, if it had happened on the street, Sabra would have been arrested. The referee showed him a red card as the Lebanese team manager grabbed him and dragged him to the dressing room, theatrically punching him over and over in the head to show the crowd that justice was being meted out. Remarkably it worked and the crowd calmed down. They began to chant, 'Glory, glory, Kim Jong-un.'

The game was almost over, but just as time was about to run out, Lebanon won a free kick on the left. It was played short and the captain Hassan Maatouk fired a hopeful, dipping shot from an improbable angle. The North Korean players stood still and watched the ball. The goalkeeper seemed to be bamboozled, losing the flight of the ball, until it nestled into the back of the net. There was silence as the referee blew his whistle. The game had somehow finished 2-2 and the North Korea fans filed out as orderly and quietly as they had arrived.

I'd later meet Jørn Andersen at the Koryo Hotel where he was rewatching the match in the revolving restaurant on the top floor. 'It was very quiet after the game,' he says of the atmosphere in the dressing room. 'They were disappointed too. After 60 minutes every player knows they have to play 90 minutes. They are very tired.' Andersen manages to be both blunt and articulate, friendly and wary at the same time. He had come in for a lot of criticism in Norway for taking the job in the first place. He was unhappy with two interviews he did which he says painted him in a bad light. He records our talk, just in case. 'It is very clean here. It is very quiet. Not many cars. It is very easy to live here,' he says. 'There's no pressure from the press. No people speak to you about football.'

The next day, there would be no mention in the state media of the ball-boy incident and only a small mention of the match itself. *Rodong Sinmun* ran a short match report. It read, 'Both sides tried their best. With strategic works, there was the correct connection when it came to kicking the ball. Both teams attacked their goals and there was a late strike. It was a good game. The result was 2-2.'

* * *

After a week of having a minder everywhere I went, and a constant low-level fear that I might be arrested at any moment if the North Korean regime decided it might be useful to have a Western journalist as a bargaining chip, I was ready to leave for the relative freedom of China. The Lebanese team are already at the departure terminal of the Pyongyang International Airport, again incongruous in their bright red training tops with 'LEBANON' written on the back. Omar Bugiel's mind is now thinking about this Saturday's League Two match. 'We've got Exeter City Saturday but I don't think I'll play,' he says, sadly. He was worried that his coach at Forest Green Rovers would be upset that he had travelled all this way not to play. 'I couldn't sleep the first few days either,' he says. 'I hope he won't be too angry.'

Regardless of not playing, the trip had been great for team morale. But he was ready for home. 'I can't wait to get back and have a full English and a big cup of tea, get into my car and then drive on a motorway,' he says, suddenly sounding like the most English man on earth. Despite the 30-hour flight home, Omar came on as a late substitute against Exeter City, and set up the consolation goal in a 3-1 defeat.

The return match in Beirut a few weeks later would not go well for North Korea, who lost 5-0. Eventually the two postponed games against Malaysia were rescheduled to be played at a neutral venue, a few days apart. The remote Thai town of Buriram was chosen. In an empty Thunder Castle Stadium – home to Thai league giants Buriram United FC – North Korea won both games 4-1. It would come down to the last group match against Hong Kong, which North Korea won 2-0. Both North Korea and Lebanon qualified for the tournament, but Andersen quit straight after the Hong Kong game (to take up a job in South Korea) while neither Soony nor Omar made it to Lebanon's 2019 Asian Cup squad. Coincidentally the two teams were drawn in the same group but went out in the group stage. When they played each other in the final game, a dead rubber, Lebanon won 4-1.

Perhaps more importantly, nuclear war was avoided. There was a war of words. President Trump called Kim Jong-un 'little rocket man' while threatening to destroy North Korea. Kim Jong-un retorted by calling Trump a 'frightened dog' and a 'dotard'. But then an unlikely bromance flourished. The two met three times – in Singapore, Vietnam and at the DMZ between North and South Korea, which my guide had taken me to after the Lebanon game. The talks didn't seem to deter Kim Jong-un's nuclear ambitions though. In October 2020 a huge military parade was held at Kim Il-sung Square, to mark the 75th anniversary of the founding of the ruling Workers' Party. Kim Jong-un stood on the same long dais that I had walked past, and watched the world's largest intercontinental ballistic missile roll past. 'Should anyone undermine our national security and mobilise military power against us, I will retaliate by using the most powerful offensive force at our disposal and in a pre-emptive manner,' Kim Jong-un was quoted as saying.

That, however, was all to come. Back in Pyongyang the North Korean soldiers checked every pocket and bag looking for books and USBs, anything that might bring prohibited reading material or films *out* of the country. All the Lebanese players were there including Maher Sabra, who had been given the red card for his altercation with a ball boy from the Pyongyang International Football School. I was worried he might have been arrested. 'He lost his head a bit!' says Soony, who had only been on the pitch for a few minutes before the incident happened. 'He kicked the ball and missed him. He would have taken his head off if he'd connected.'

After a week of living in an alternative reality, Soony now had a long flight back to Kansas. 'I'm just glad to be going home,' he says. 'And I'm done with politics.' With that, the last American in Pyongyang boarded his plane home.

I've Come Home
by Nick Ames

Iceland v Kosovo
World Cup qualifier
Reykjavík, Iceland
10 October 2017

The people of Reykjavík wanted to see the most successful sportsmen Iceland has produced, but instead they were treated to a confused English journalist and his two colleagues. I was in the middle of a stage at one end of Ingólfstorg Square, in the middle of the country's capital, and thousands of nonplussed faces looked back. The perils of taking a wrong turn can lead you into surprising situations; I took a quick photo, half waved awkwardly and scurried back behind the curtain before anyone could ask too many questions.

Moments later a gate opened to the left and now, after the completely unwanted warm-up act, up came the night's superstars. Iceland's footballers had just reached world football's pinnacle and they were ready to play all the old crowd-pleasers. The 'thunderclap' that had been heard round the world from 2016? Go on then. A vigorous dancing session led by a renowned local rapper? Sure. Watching from the side, by now, the only cogent thought was that it would be nice if, somehow, the party could last forever; a moment in history, an unrepeatable and completely surprising one of sheer joy and innocence, stretching out as far as your eyes could see.

That would have been greedy because, three days previously, the vision had hardly been conceivable at all. The journey here had begun somewhere in the depths of Norfolk. For a freelance football journalist, international breaks count as lifeblood: somewhere, often a cheapish flight away from you, a story is being told that reinforces football's inextricable relationship with history, geopolitics and the sheer power of human will. Those are often the tales that are not covered by writers on the Premier League beat, who quite rightly relish a breather: that fortnight early in September, October or November offers a chance to put stories less told in the spotlight; it brings promise of adventure and, almost inevitably, rapid changes of plan.

In October 2017, though, I was staying in England. There was not an obvious story among the two remaining rounds of UEFA's World Cup qualifying fixtures, or at least one that justified taking a chance on. A group of old friends had hired a house in Cromer for the weekend so, via two trains from London, I was on my way to make at least some amends for years of no-shows or last-minute apologies. Between conversation with my travelling companions, my eyes glanced furtively down to the screen of my phone. Could something, just perhaps, happen in Group I?

I had covered Iceland's qualification for Euro 2016, visited the country for a week before the tournament, spent time at their base camp in Annecy at the finals in France and then been present in Nice when they beat England on one of the most gripping football nights I will ever experience. You become drawn into long-term stories like this one; you make friends, forge relationships, harbour sincere affection for the people who have afforded you a glimpse into their lives. If Iceland reached the World Cup for the first time, a country of 350,000 achieving something genuinely incredible, I was determined to be there both for professional pride and the sense of responsibility you feel to see a story through.

There was little chance of it happening this month though. They sat behind Croatia, the group leaders who occupied the only automatic slot, on goal difference with two games to play; that might sound tight but, given Croatia were playing an insipid Finland at home while Iceland visited Turkey – a mercurial side who needed a win – the chances were it would be all over by the end of the journey to East Anglia.

Not necessarily. Iceland put in another of their monumental efforts in the Turkish city of Eskişehir and, by the time the train had passed Ipswich, they were three goals up. There was half an hour left and Croatia had just scored too, as expected; at least Iceland should make the play-offs now, which would hopefully mean a reporting trip in November.

The journey rattled on beyond Diss and the night was pitch black now, little visible bar the outlines of trees flanking the railway line. Then something remarkable happened. In Rijeka, a little-known Finnish midfielder called Pyry Soiri had capitalised on Croatia's inability to defend a bouncing ball and, with a minute to play, blasted high into Danijel Subašić's goal. It was enough to make you sit bolt upright in the hard, knobbly Greater Anglia standard-class seat. If Finland could see out the added time, Iceland would only need a home win over Kosovo to make it to Russia 2018 in three days' time.

Finland did it, and now the questions were simple: could I get to Reykjavík before Monday afternoon without breaking the bank? Would my old friends at the Iceland FA be able to fix accreditation for the biggest match their country had ever hosted? Would both the editors I worked for take articles from a game that, unless the rock-bottom Kosovans pulled out something improbable themselves, would be the week's most significant in sport? Could I arrange most of this in the next half hour and be mentally 'present' for a weekend in which I had promised myself – and others – football would not be a factor?

I landed in Iceland a little after 8am on Monday, the sun still rising to the west. It was misty and I thought of the last time I had arrived here, in April 2016, when the sky was brighter and the frontiers entirely new. After a few days in Reykjavík, I had flown, in a tiny 18-seater, to meet Heimir Hallgrímsson on the tiny island of Heimaey. Hallgrímsson was co-manager of Iceland at the time, an unusual arrangement that seemed to fit the country's approach to success both on the football pitch and elsewhere.

'Meet me at the airport and I'll give you the grand tour,' he had written over e-mail the previous week. Like every Icelander I have met, Hallgrímsson was as good as his word. If the drive around Heimaey, a 5.2-square-mile protrusion of rock that had been both engulfed and completely reshaped by a volcanic explosion in 1973, did not take especially long then there was plenty to focus on within.

For many years Hallgrímsson's career had been modest, spent largely on Heimaey with the men's and women's teams of the island's club, IBV Vestmannaeyjar, until he had formally joined the national team's set-up – initially as an assistant in 2011 before joining Lars Lagerback as joint coach for the Euro 2016 qualifying campaign. All the way through he had worked as the local dentist while coaching. Even now, when we met, he had appointments in the diary and he led me through a fully equipped surgery en route to the top floor of his house, where his 'cognac room' boasted a 180-degree view of the island. Hallgrímsson was an exceptionally likeable figure – honest, direct and thoughtful – who had a flattering habit of working his way through questions with a consideration that suggested he had been asked to mine a previously unvisited area of the self.

He told me about *Tolfan*, the supporters' group whose interest in the national team had waned to almost zero before he had become involved in the set-up. Icelandic football had been bumping along in Europe's nether reaches, the team winning only five of

38 games in their qualifiers for World Cup 2006, Euro 2008, World Cup 2010 and Euro 2012. Hallgrímsson decided, before a friendly with the Faroe Islands in August 2012, to pick things up. He would meet with the fans in Ölver, a pub close to the national stadium, and shatter any barriers between the national team set-up and its support.

'I told them that, before every home game, I would go in there two, two and a half hours before kick-off and give them a report into what we were going to do,' he said. 'They would be the first to know the starting XI. For the game against the Faroes, maybe ten or 12 people came. I told them the team, described how we would play, showed them the motivational video we had made for the players and made sure they were watching it at the same time as the team.

'These days I go there at the same time, whatever the fixture, and there are around 400 fans in there. It's really unusual that a national coach would turn up before a game like this, perhaps sweet in a way, silly too because there could always be a drunk guy who knocks me cold or whatever. But this is Iceland – we dare to be a little bit different.'

Now I would see that for myself. Hallgrímsson had taken the reins solo from Lagerback, the vastly experienced Swede, after the quarter-final finish in

Euro 2016. Plenty of friends and relatives had told him not to do it; that the chances of doing it all again were too slim and the potential downsides overly steep. So it was a vindication of his understated but fierce self-belief that, outside Ölver, the crowds were queuing in the damp to witness his most significant address yet.

'If I see any phones, they'll be flushed down the toilet,' an MC warned those who made it inside. The code of secrecy around these meetings was strict and, incredibly given the numbers and the temptation to make a short-term name for oneself on social media, strictly adhered to every time. That was the bargain the nation and its football coach had struck.

There were plenty of drunk men and women in the room but nothing but unremitting love for Hallgrímsson, who was cheered to the rafters when he entered shortly after 4pm. His very presence held the audience captive: nobody else said a word over the next 25 minutes, in which he explained how Iceland would beat Kosovo, what the potential banana skins might be, and shared the presentation he had devised for the team. It felt like being let in on a secret society, most of its members clad in blue shirts with Sigurðsson, Bjarnason or Sigþórsson printed on the back. Now the society knew what was in store, it was back to the beers and then, with Hallgrímsson long gone, on at last to Laugardalsvöllur.

I had been to Laugardalsvöllur once before, but never to watch a football match. It is a small, essentially two-sided ground set in a dip to the east of the city centre. Its grounds manager, Kristinn Johannsson, was an acquaintance through mutual friends in London and he had taken me around his pride and joy in 2016 – explaining the pitfalls behind attempting to maintain an international-quality surface in a part of the world prone to such harsh, capricious seasonal weather. 'See that ice?' he had asked, pointing to a picture in his office beneath the main stand, taken in February 2014, that showed the pitch covered in what resembled a white sheet. 'It's between eight and ten centimetres thick. That's what we are dealing with year in, year out.'

Preparing for an October showdown felt like comparative child's play to Johannsson given, in 2013, he had readied the surface for a November World Cup play-off against Croatia. Iceland had never hosted an international game that late in the year. He did his side of the job and the team almost did theirs, but a goalless draw on that freezing night was followed by a 2-0 defeat in Zagreb four days later. It was the moment Iceland first held the global attention for footballing reasons; the fact there was more to tell four years later

211

was testament to a phenomenal collective effort, based on peerless youth and coach development.

This was their chance to exact revenge, for however short a time, over the Croatians but most importantly to make their own dreams come true. The previous year I had met up with Gunnleifur Gunnleifsson, a veteran goalkeeper who won 26 caps for Iceland and – remarkably – was still playing in the local league late in 2020 at the age of 45. Gunnleifsson remembered watching a rare 4-0 win over Liechtenstein in 1998 that drew only 550 supporters to Laugardalsvöllur; he recalled 'training in a room used for horse shows' with his semi-professional club side, 'playing on gravel, horse shit, all that.' Indoor halls became crucial to Iceland's football development, given that outside pitches were near unplayable for much of the year, but over the previous decade and a half the facilities had become highly specialised, many in number and influential in the fact almost 22,000 Icelanders were now registered footballers.

Here, in the increasingly chilly and windswept outdoors, 11 of them would look to execute Hallgrímsson's game plan. I walked the short distance from Ölver and entered Laugardalsvöllur, where I immediately bumped into a confused-looking friend and colleague from Kosovo. I had been following

Kosovo, too, since their first official international in 2014, also covering their inaugural 2018 World Cup qualifier – in Finland, where I watched them earn a point – and felt comfortable around their national team entourage. This time they were not the story, although they certainly had the potential to scupper it: even if they were far behind Iceland's curve in terms of organisation and finances, Kosovo had a squad of technical, attacking players who should grace a major tournament themselves before too long. They were understandably raw and had not taken a single point since holding the Finns in Turku, but in players like Milot Rashica and Bersant Celina they had creative forces who could easily spoil the party if Iceland were a few degrees short of their characteristic intensity.

The sky was a foreboding, awesome shade of grey as the match kicked off. There were just shy of 10,000 inside Laugardalsvöllur this time, bucking any tired clichés of Nordic reserve and making enough noise to ensure the sound did not carry straight out of the open ends. Iceland were as skittish as anyone might have expected for an occasion of this size. They had secured their passage to Euro 2016 with a nervy goalless home draw against Kazakhstan – a poor result in isolation but, in those circumstances, enough to win the ticket. That would not be enough this time unless Croatia, needing to win against a Ukraine side that were not completely out of the picture themselves, fell short too.

Rashica almost scored for Kosovo from range and, as half-time approached, Iceland had barely opened their opponents up. Then they received a helping hand. Messy Kosovo defending saw the ball squirt to Gylfi Sigurðsson. It had to be Sigurðsson, the undoubted star in an otherwise largely unheralded set of individuals, who produced Iceland's big moment. Shaping to shoot with his left foot, he instead brought the ball inside and, via a ricochet off the defender his swerve had nutmegged, found himself clean through 12 yards out. He made no mistake from there and, for the next minute or so, the number of voices inside the national stadium seemed to have multiplied by a dozen.

The remainder of the match was relatively serene, Kosovo's neat probing rarely generating anything that might bother a robust, supremely drilled Iceland defence. The roof, such as it was, lifted off its fittings again with 22 minutes left when Sigurðsson got away down the left, created space and then centred low for a sliding Jóhann Berg Guðmundsson, the Burnley winger, to jab in the goal that eliminated any shadow of doubt.

Hallgrímsson punched the air and joined his staff in a celebratory bundle while his players did exactly the same on Johannsson's perfectly manicured green turf. The latter stages were played out as if in a haze; everyone knew what was coming and, a little before 8.45pm local time, Iceland's first World Cup finals appearance was confirmed.

On a selfish level it vindicated the journey – the dash back to London from north-east Norfolk only 24 hours previously and the 2.30am wake-up call that meant it was time to stumble into the taxi to Luton airport. I thought back four years to a similar, if lengthier, assignment I had undertaken in 2013 – travelling from Sarajevo to Kaunas with fans of Bosnia-Herzegovina in order to see whether their side would win in Lithuania and reach their own maiden World Cup. That night, unwelcome depths of creativity would have been required to push any articles through had Vedad Ibišević not illuminated a dull game by scoring in the 68th minute – exactly the same time at which Guðmundsson made sure for Iceland. Any excursion of this nature put you, necessarily, on a wing and a prayer: this one had worked out perfectly but, as I tried in vain to thaw my hands in order to begin typing, the only feelings of joy were for the remarkable set of players, coaches, backroom staff and fans I had got to know – if only in a small way – over the previous year and a half.

One thing I had not known until the post-match celebrations in Nice – when my excitement, despite being an Englishman, at what I had just witnessed led me to giddily hug Hallgrímsson in the mixed zone – was the importance of the local folk song 'Ég Er Kominn Heim' ('I've Come Home'). It was adapted from an old Hungarian tune and is now something of an unofficial Icelandic anthem. Played in conjunction with thousands of swaying, singing blue shirts it is an almost impossibly moving assault on the senses; on the Cote d'Azur it had played long into the night and here, while everyone connected with the team lined up with arms around one another on the pitch to savour what had just passed, it played again while Laugardalsvöllur reverberated to its melody.

This is what you watch football for, I thought: for those moments of almost sublime human connection that far transcend who did what, when and where on the pitch. Given Iceland's size, how could this not be a victory for everyone in the country; of the battles against the elements, bigger neighbours and infinitely more storied football teams that had marked their history? 'An Icelander is never satisfied,' Arnar Bill Gunnarsson, the local FA's technical director, had told me a few yards from my press-box seat in a plush meeting room back in 2015.

'He wants more and won't ever give up. That's how we are conditioned.'

All that was left to fight over now, for most of those present, was Reykjavík's stock of alcohol. I finished my short-term working commitments and then jumped in a taxi with Stan Collymore, the former Liverpool forward who was helming a documentary show for Russia Today, and his crew in a bid to beat Hallgrímsson and his players to the city centre. We made it to Ingólfstorg, pressed our credentials home to a squad of burly security guards, and disappeared backstage before our brief moment as unexpected local celebrities; by now I was running purely on adrenaline. Iceland's greatest night still had adventures in store, because you only qualify for your first World Cup once after all.

The music played on, the stories told in Reykjavík's bars became taller, but one incontrovertible fact remained: Iceland, minuscule Iceland, had reached the World Cup. The next morning, mildly hungover and eating fresh cod in a cafe on trendy Skólavörðustígur, I reflected that I had been guzzling crabmeat in Cromer around 40 hours before. It is what football does to you and what, for all the trauma the world has undergone in 2020, it will do many times all over again.

The Final Final
by Martino Simcik Arese

Boca Juniors v River Plate
Copa Libertadores Final
Buenos Aires, Argentina
11 November 2018

Let me start this tale near the end. It's 25 November, a few hours before the second leg of the final of the century. I'm in Buenos Aires standing outside the Monumental, River Plate's iconic stadium. Rocks are hitting the team bus of Boca Juniors. Tear gas has been fired.

Chaos then followed. The game Argentina had waited a lifetime for was suddenly in jeopardy. No one knew what was going on although we knew things had gone to shit when we found ourselves chasing Gianni Infantino, FIFA's president, down the tunnel to demand why was he leaving before the game of games had even kicked off. The sight of Infantino scurrying away told us what we needed to know even if the news hadn't reached the rest of the city. Outside the ground, families were still being robbed of their tickets but it would be another five hours until the 2019 Copa Libertadores Final was officially cancelled. How on earth did we get to this?

Twenty days earlier the stage was set for a momentous occasion. The game of the century: River Plate versus Boca Juniors in the Copa Libertadores Final. A super *superclasico*. In the semi-finals Boca had defeated an impressive Palmeiras, while River Plate controversially squeezed through 2-2 on aggregate over Grêmio. River Plate's coach Marcelo Gallardo had been banned from communicating with his players after receiving a red card in the previous match. However, at half-time of the second leg he had snuck into River's locker room to give a rousing speech, which caused Grêmio to appeal the result. It was all in vain. Nothing was stopping the super *superclasico*.

I had been with COPA90 for four years, and presenter Eli Mengem and I had got to the point where we were in charge of deciding what kind of films we wanted to make. So, when word came – at 4am London time on a Thursday that we would indeed have a Boca-River final – we began building the case for us to be sent out there. It would be the last Copa Libertadores final to ever be played over two legs, home and away. It wasn't a hard case to make. By the following Tuesday at 11am we were in Buenos Aires. We had been given three weeks to capture the history, local tradition and rivalry of the two most iconic clubs in the southern hemisphere. The first notification on my phone seemed to be a portent for the days ahead, 'Boca Juniors And River Plate Fans Have Argument, Someone's House Gets Burned Down.'

Boca-River has always produced fireworks, but there was something about knockout football that brought out the worst, and sometimes the best, in everyone. In 2004 a 20-year-old Carlos Tevez scored an 88th-minute goal in a Copa Libertadores semi-final, and was promptly sent off for mocking the seething Monumental with his 'chicken dance'. Boca have used the nickname *gallina*, the Spanish for chicken, ever since River dramatically lost the 1966 Copa Libertadores final 4-2 to Peñarol, despite being 2-0 up at half-time.

Boca went on to lose the 2004 final but the only thing that mattered was the Tevez dance that almost sparked a riot. In 2015, Boca Juniors faced elimination during a round of 16 match. At half-time, with the River Plate players about to leave the tunnel of Boca's famous La Bombonera, a fan released pepper spray.

Four River players were taken to hospital, the match was abandoned, and Boca were kicked out of the competition. Historically, the two are level on the big stage, with one exception. River Plate's infamous relegation in 2011, something that has come to define the culture of banter, or *cargadas*, that can be particularly pointed in Argentina. This time the incidents would carry a bigger weight. One that extends beyond the confines of the stadium, and even football itself.

Our crew in Buenos Aires was made up of seven people: two cameramen, two local producers, myself, Eli and Pepe Perretta. Pepe was an artist renowned for creating many of the greatest *telones* in Argentina and around the world – those huge, ornate and highly artistic flags and banners you see covering whole stands. Pepe is in his 40s and covered in tattoos. He has a big beard, loves heavy metal and drives a Harley. He's the kind of larger than life personality that makes you think you're in a movie when you're around him. From his years of experience making banners and artwork for Argentina's *barras bravas*, the hardcore organised fan groups which control the country's stadiums, he had a direct line to every major terrace leader in South America.

First up was the home leg in Boca's home, La Bombonera. Press passes, we discovered, were impossible to find, and tickets were going for around $3,000 each, so we had to find alternative routes. After a few phone calls we found a back door and slipped in late as a guest of one of the sponsors. We arrived at the ground on the morning of 10 November, the intended day of the game, to a torrential downpour. Despite 12 hours of continuous rain the neighbourhood of La Boca was as crowded as ever. The streets rang out with what had become their unofficial chant of the match:

> *I love you Boca Juniors*
> *I love you truly*
> *I want the Libertadores*
> *And to kill a chicken*

The streets were flooded, up to our knees in some parts, but the air was filled with the hypnotic noise of *himnos* and the smell of *churrascarias*, a type of Argentine BBQ. Everyone seemed to be drinking the Argentine street drink of choice: Fernet-Branca and cola, poured into a half-cut plastic bottle.

As Eli and some of the crew packed into a flooded Bombonera, I jumped on the back of Pepe's Harley and made my way across town to the Monumental where thousands of River fans were waiting to send their team off. There, among a sea of red and white, Pepe helped me slip through to where the main leaders of River's *barra* were gathered. Inevitably, on River's side of town, the people we spoke to gleefully derided Boca Juniors for their flooded ground. There was a class element to it all. Both River and Boca came from La Boca, the working-class port-side neighbourhood. But River soon jumped ship and set up home in the wealthier northern suburbs of Buenos Aires. Their newly salubrious home, plus a string of world record transfer fees in the 1930s, is why River fans started calling themselves *Los Millonarios*. Boca, meanwhile, are referred to as *bosteros*, or shit collectors, a reference to the working-class nature of the neighbourhood they left behind. News came through that the flooding at La Bombonera, Boca's pride and joy, was so bad the match was called off. As one River fan told me, 'Once again, they [Boca] are the shame of Argentina.' The match was postponed to the following day.

The next morning, we began seeing news stories speculating on what any further delay might mean for the final. A week after the second leg was scheduled to take place, Buenos Aires was hosting the G20 summit. Argentina's president at the time, Mauricio Macri, was the former president of Boca Juniors. With an impending election the following year, the final was meant to be a defining moment for him, proving that Argentina could properly host a two-legged Copa

Libertadores final and then a successful summit. It was to become the great test, and legacy, of his presidency. Macri had initially intended to allow away supporters at each leg, a requirement in the Copa Libertadores. The authorities quickly scrapped the idea. After all, due to the violence, Boca-River had not seen away fans in the league for over two decades. Starting now, with the stakes so high, seemed unlikely.

We split into two teams. Eli and most of the crew would film inside the grounds. I would run around town with Pepe, capturing the opposing fans' reactions. Pepe and I headed out to capture the buzz with the River supporters. We would first head to the Monumental for a second attempt at capturing the *bandierazo*, or send-off. We'd then watch the match, in the neighbourhood of Moron, with a local fan club. Just like the previous day, fans were out in their thousands by 9am for a match scheduled to kick off at 4pm.

Shortly after kick-off, Eli messaged to say he had just witnessed the greatest atmosphere of his life. At the Bombonera, Ramón Ábila had put Boca ahead. The railing from the second ring of the ground was ripped out in celebration, only for River Plate to score a minute later. In the second half Darío Benedetto netted a second for Boca. At the Moron clubhouse you could hear a pin drop. For the first 45 minutes I was huddled under a TV as the small pub packed with River Plate faithful belted out chants and hurled abuse at the screen. One old man caught my eye. He had kept his index and middle finger crossed for the entire half, not even breaking to take a swig of his beer.

The second half was more of the same and he never broke the knot except for the 61st minute, when River equalised with thanks to an own goal from Boca's Carlos Izquierdoz. I was drenched in a mix of cola, Fernet-Branca and beer. It finished 2-2. The River Plate fans in Moron were happy with the two away goals. Pepe and I hugged our new friends who had given me a dry shirt of their local bar, hopped on his Harley and made our way back to the neighbourhood of Palermo.

We spent the weeks that followed interviewing different characters in the city. A few stood out. There was Lito Costa Febre, River Plate's famed match commentator. He became known around the world for his impassioned speech as River Plate were sent down to the second division and has since become an idol to fans of his club. We sat with him at his radio booth and when asked what he would do after the game, he simply answered, 'I will be walking 70km to the chapel of my patron saint. Either to give thanks for this moment of unprecedented joy or pray for strength to endure the pain of such painful defeat.'

Then there was Diego, a local cab driver and diehard Boca Juniors fan with a crucifix and a small photo of Riquelme hanging from his mirror. We met him ahead of the first leg. He told us how he was planning to miss the baptism of his niece to catch the match. After the torrential rain and the draw the following day, we took another ride with him. He was convinced Boca would win. 'God brought the rain so I could attend the baptism,' he said. 'God supports Boca.'

On two separate evenings ahead of what was meant to be the final leg, we went to two barbecues. The first was with a group of Boca fans from Villa Lugano, a working-class housing estate on the south side of the city. The second, with the River fans I had met the previous match day in the suburb of Moron. Both sets of supporters knew we were making a documentary, and nothing had been pre-arranged, yet the two experiences eerily mirrored each other. Grilled meat, Quilmes by the litre, and families showing us their newborns, each with club membership cards made on the day of their births. On the Boca side they also prepared roasted chickens, presented to us adorned in a River Plate scarf, referencing the *Cargada* of *Las Gallinas*. On the River Plate side, it was a suckling pig draped in a Carlos Tevez shirt, a nod to the title, *Los Bosteros*.

The *himnos* rang out, a solitary trumpet on both sides leading identical melodies.

On 22 November, two days ahead of the final, Boca Juniors decided to hold an open training session at La Bombonera. No tickets were required, I had been told. It was a strictly first-come, first-served basis. I arrived at the stadium 30 minutes before the training was meant to start, naively believing I might be able to squeeze in. By the time I reached the ground the queues had already grown violent. The 49,000-capacity stadium was packed with an estimated 60,000 supporters. Another 20,000, at least, were outside fighting for their chance to get in. The police pepper-sprayed the crowd to try and push them back.

After failing to get in at two entrances, and after helping lift women and children out of the packed crowds, I hopped a fence to the media entrance. There I miraculously found myself in front of a Brazilian television crew that I had met the previous year at the Camp Nou while covering Neymar's transfer from Barcelona to PSG. They agreed to tell the local security that I was part of the crew. Just as most training sessions in front of supporters, this was little more than an exercise in trying to motivate the players. The Bombonera was electrifying. One fan managed to invade the pitch and reach Tevez who saved him from being trampled by police. The Boca players even let him join in on a game of rondo before being applauded off the pitch.

The chaos outside the ground was all over the news. Boca's poor organisation meant that Mauricio Macri banned Boca from being able to take a celebratory lap in front of their fans at La Bombonera, in case of a victory. Traditionally this would be done in the stadium where a team wins, but with no away support, and an infamous precedent from 1969 where Boca only made it halfway around the ground after winning the league title at the Monumental, this was out of the question. It was clear that the situation was far from under control. The football world's eyes were focused on Buenos Aires. But there was a surprise around every corner.

The next morning I received a call from Pepe. One of the leaders of River Plate's *barra* had narrowly escaped arrest. But he was carrying over £200,000 in cash and 300 tickets for the final, which were promptly confiscated. The police had clearly been tipped off, and rumours began to spread that the *barra* would take revenge for what had been done. In Argentina, the *barras bravas*, particularly when it comes to the more successful clubs, are often closely connected to the presidents who run them. Boca's *barra*, *La Doce*, famously helped campaign for Mauricio Macri's successful campaign to be elected president of the club. He would later become mayor of Buenos Aires and then president of Argentina. Among the gossip and intrigue found in the release of US diplomatic cables by Wikileaks, one document details a meeting between the US ambassador and Macri, who claimed that running Boca provided an 'outstanding political education'.

We woke up on the morning of 24 November, aware that anything could happen. Although I had a plan to follow. I was to ride with Pepe to collect footage to be sent back to London, attend the pre-match event organised by a sponsor, report for CNN if anything happened that was newsworthy, and then eventually head to La Boca to capture Boca Juniors' supporters before they left. The rest of the crew would be in the ground to film what we hoped would be a historic match. As we reached the Monumental, Pepe parked down the block from where the Boca Juniors bus was meant to reach the ground.

The area was teeming with River Plate fans, just as in the first leg. Fans had arrived hours before, many without tickets. It was tense. Inside, the Monumental was a buzz of activity. But the real action that would define the tie was outside when Boca's bus started getting pelted by bottles. A row of about 20 police officers wildly pepper-sprayed anyone nearby, whether they had thrown a bottle or not, as the bus sped behind the stadium gates. Later we would learn that several of Boca's players had inhaled the gas and needed medical treatment. I called Eli inside the stadium to let him know something had gone horribly wrong. For a good 20 minutes he was the only person aware that the match was at risk of being cancelled as rumours began spreading throughout the stadium.

When I reached Pepe we got on his bike to make our way to the local TV station to send the footage back to London. On the way we saw groups of young people trying to rob passersby for their tickets. 'They are not in the *barra*,' Pepe noticed. 'Neither were the people who attacked the bus, I mean who knows exactly what is happening, this is Argentina. Maybe the police have done this to make the case for an increase in pensions.'

After sending the footage and reaching La Boca, there was nothing but confusion. CNN began ringing me every hour to ask for an update, but there was nothing to clearly report. Who was responsible? It could have been anyone; the *barra*, the police, the president of one of the clubs? Macri himself? The conspiracy theories were wild. Even if the most likely explanation was the simplest. Pure ineptitude.

So what's happened with the game? Eventually, after about six hours of confusion, and after a riot at the Monumental, the match was cancelled. At first there was hope that the game could be played the following day. We waited in front of the TV for a final decision from CONMEBOL, South American football's governing body. After about two hours, with about 20,000 people already in and around River Plate's stadium, the game was officially called off. Initially it was postponed until after the G20 summit, pending a court case. The match of the century had grown too big, the stakes too high. That night, we made our way to a Racing Club de Avellaneda game, but it couldn't fill the hole that the aborted Copa Libertadores final had left. We would be leaving Buenos Aires after three weeks with everything still in the balance.

We called Diego the taxi driver to make our way to the airport and return to London. Diego was devastated, and he didn't know who to blame. 'All of this passion, all this joy, all this emotion, that is what makes us special!' he said. 'But what's the point if we can't even enjoy the festival. At this point I've lost all interest.' As tears streamed down his face, I realised that in essence the game was dead. In the coming weeks, Diego's words would come to ring even truer. The final leg was eventually assigned to Madrid. It was the final insult. The match would take place thousands of miles away, excluding the majority of fans. Worse still, the competition named in honour of those who had freed the continent from colonial rule would be decided in the capital of Argentina's former coloniser.

In the end I attended the match in Madrid as well. Spain has the largest Argentine diaspora in the world, but the atmosphere was flat. It was nothing like what I had experienced the previous month. River won 3-1, but it was merely a formality. It was supposed to be the greatest game ever played, the super *superclasico*. Instead, it was an ending, the final final, and a shame that no one would ever be able to wash.

The Battle of Valenciennes
by Molly Hudson

England v Cameroon
Women's World Cup finals
Valenciennes, France
23 June 2019

Following England at a World Cup is an experience like no other. For many of the journalists and fans who travelled to France to follow England it was their first taste of a Women's World Cup and proved to carry many of the hallmarks of a traditional England tournament experience; hope, growing expectations that ultimately exceeded performance, before unceremoniously crashing out of the tournament via a penalty kick.

But even for those seasoned reporters that had witnessed heartbreak and drama on a scale that only England can produce, 23 June 2019 will live long in the memory. It was once described as 'the single most anarchic game' in the national team's history.

To understand the importance of England's round of 16 game against Cameroon, we must travel back to January 2018 and the announcement of former Manchester United defender Phil Neville as the Lionesses' head coach, following the departure of previous manager Mark Sampson. A figure as widely recognisable as Neville brought a spotlight on results that the women's game had never seen before. It also brought criticism of the Football Association, and their appointment of a manager that had no coaching experience in the women's game, and little in the men's. For his part, Neville wholeheartedly bought into the role. His sister Tracey Neville excelled in women's netball which, he had said, helped him to understand the unique balance of growing a game in participation terms as well as its on-pitch success.

'Management is all-encompassing,' said Phil Neville. 'That's something I've learned since starting this job. I find it very difficult to switch off. I can be at the cinema or out for a meal with my wife and I'm thinking constantly about what my players are doing. How are they playing? Are they fit? Are they doing their recovery?' Taking England to the Women's World Cup, he said, was the biggest moment in his professional life. 'Tracey was right: this is the biggest and best thing I have ever done. It's the absolute pinnacle for me. I can't wait to stand on that touchline.'

His first year was spent getting to know the team, exploring his managerial ideas and formations. By the 2019 SheBelieves Cup, a friendly tournament between England and three teams then ranked in the FIFA top ten – hosts USA were the best in the world, Japan were eighth and Brazil tenth – the team's form appeared to be coming together. They lifted their first trophy under Neville – beating Japan and Brazil and drawing with the US – sparking praise for the winning mentality that his side had begun to cultivate.

England landed in France with an expectation that they could realistically win the competition, with Neville and his players talking of dethroning the holders USA. They faced a group including Japan, Scotland and tournament debutants Argentina. England came through the games unscathed, unbeaten and most importantly undeterred from their goal of becoming champions. By winning their group, they achieved a favourable tie in Valenciennes, a sleepy town in northern France, against Cameroon, who had finished in third place in Group E, needing a dramatic 95th-minute winner from striker Ajara Nchout against New Zealand to progress to the knockout round.

Known as the Indomitable Lionesses, Cameroon were appearing at their second World Cup having lost 1-0 to China in the 2015 edition in Canada and appearing at the London 2012 Olympics. Seeded 43 places below England in the FIFA world rankings, Cameroon were clear underdogs. Much of the pre-match build-up centred around which of Neville's players may line up against Cameroon as the England manager heavily rotated his squad for the three group games. But there was an intriguing subplot – the Video Assistant Referee.

The tournament was using VAR and its new interpretation of the laws of the game, which had only been introduced at the beginning of June, the same month the World Cup began. Emma Hayes, the Chelsea manager, articulated the feelings of many that the women's game was being used as a guinea pig ahead of the wider implementation of VAR in the Premier League the following season.

'Yes, these are the rules but I just do not think it is right to introduce new ones on 1 June, a week before the tournament starts, and expect elite players in the games of their lives to have to adapt that quickly, especially when even the slightest breach is now being picked up by VAR,' Hayes wrote in a column in *The Times*. 'I know these rules apply across the global game, but this is the Women's World Cup – which is by far the most high-profile tournament, the pinnacle, of the summer. It is no place for experiments, or to treat the women as guinea pigs. Sadly, that still happens.' She ended her column with a foreboding statement. 'With so much good football already, and more to come, I just pray that we do not end up getting wound up by VAR.'

Having travelled from Nice to Le Havre and back in the group stages, England enjoyed the relative peace and quiet of Valenciennes. It was a warm French summer and the players and their families were relaxed and at ease enough to enjoy coffee in the main square on the morning of the game in relative anonymity. The walk to Stade du Hainaut from the town centre offered travelling fans a sense of the tournament. The flags of England and Cameroon adorned local pubs and restaurants. There was a feeling, belatedly, that France was beginning to understand the importance of a tournament that appeared largely ignored in cities such as Paris.

Cameroon and their fans were anything but forgettable. They were colourful and energetic; the sense in the England camp was that this would be an exciting display of the beautiful game from two of its most football-mad continents. But beautiful it was not. As the players kicked off in the baking heat it did not take long for tempers to rise. Cameroon defender Yvonne Leuko received an early caution for a needless elbow on Nikita Parris that would set the tone for the rest of the match. Parris's scream could be heard high in the stands.

Tensions continued to rise, and inside the opening 15 minutes, England were awarded an indirect free kick for a back pass to the Cameroon goalkeeper, whose team-mates were adamant that it was merely a mis-controlled pass rather than a deliberate attempt at passing to the goalkeeper. In the aftermath, Augustine Ejangue, who had made the pass, appeared to spit on Toni Duggan. The incident was the type that looked worse with the benefit of television replays and was likely accidental. The referee, Liang Qin, appeared not to see it.

Cameroon's protests had hardly abated before England captain Steph Houghton duly stepped up to fire in the resulting free kick to give her side the lead. If it appeared both sets of players had earned a lull in play and the chance to go into half-time without further drama, then VAR had other ideas. Ellen White, who was enjoying a prolific tournament, thought she had doubled England's advantage, but the on-pitch officials ruled it out for offside. Up came the VAR screen, and down on the pitch Cameroon were in despair, as they stared at a big screen and watched the infamous lines being drawn to determine whether or not the decision was correct.

Back then, VAR was in its initial stages, and, as Hayes feared before the match, was used as a guinea pig for the marginal, toenail-width offsides we have since seen in the men's Premier League and beyond. This may not have been quite *that* close, but magnified on the big screen in the stand, the Cameroon players were adamant that the images proved the goal should have remained ruled out, while VAR rightly recommended the decision should be overturned and the goal left to stand.

It is hard to imagine, both in that moment, and now looking back, what it must have felt like as a Cameroon player to feel such indignation. To stand on the pitch, and a wider stage that they had worked to reach their entire life, and feel as though they were being cheated out of a decision. The image of a group of Cameroon players, mouths open in shock, fingers pointed to the big screen, surrounding the referee who has her finger to her ear while England players looked on in confusion, appeared in several English newspapers the next morning. What followed, however, was chaos. White had scored in first-half injury time and the Cameroon players were so angered that they did not want to leave the pitch for half-time. When they were eventually persuaded to do so by manager Alain Djeumfa, the stadium fell silent for a brief period as the events of the first half sank in.

If anyone thought that at 2-0 the controversy would subside, they were mistaken. At half-time, Djeumfa reportedly told his team that he believed the referee wanted England to win. On English television, discussions centred on whether Cameroon's players were accusing officials of racism in the tunnel, although both their players and staff later denied this. At half-time, Neville would tell broadcasters, 'We were in total control. I think at times it was a little too easy for us to control.' In purely footballing terms he was right – Cameroon had failed to take a single touch of the ball in the England penalty area. Goalkeeper Karen Bardsley didn't have a save to make. But it came across as arrogant. This was a World Cup knockout round, and Cameroon were there on merit.

Appearing to have used the first-half controversy to fuel a desire to overturn the perceived injustice, Cameroon began with a renewed energy. England were carved open far too easily, and Gabrielle Onguéné picked out Ajara Nchout in the box. The midfielder thought she had scored but a VAR review showed that Onguéné was just offside and the goal was ruled out.

It was another marginal, although correct, decision followed by Cameroonian protests. This time Nchout was in tears, Djeumfa forcibly preventing her from leaving the pitch, before the rest of her team-mates too threatened to walk off.

By this point the atmosphere in the stadium had changed to something I had never experienced, and even now is hard to describe. There was a sense of unpredictability and even the Cameroon players themselves appeared unsure of how to proceed. Our Cameroon counterparts in the press box were almost as furious as the players, and like all of us unsure of the VAR rules, while the crowd had begun to boo and whistle. As play eventually continued, England began to give up chances at will, and Bardsley was called into action on several occasions to preserve her clean sheet.

England managed to add a third as Alex Greenwood scored from a Duggan corner. With 58 minutes on the clock, England were 3-0 up, having scored three goals for the first time in a knockout game at a World Cup. They were keeping their heads, while everyone around them was losing theirs. Midfielder Jill Scott would later reveal they had prepared them for crucial moments in knockout football using tips from their team psychologist.

The game was now won, but that only added to Cameroonian frustration, and the remaining half-hour would descend into an even uglier affair. By the 74th minute, Nchout had sent defender Millie Bright flying into touch with a late tackle. Lucy Staniforth and Leah Williamson were then handed their World Cup debuts, a day they are unlikely to forget for more than the usual reasons.

Fran Kirby was soon upended in the penalty area, and despite it initially appearing the referee had pointed to the penalty spot, VAR intervened and determined play could continue. There was now a growing feeling in the stands, on the pitch and in the press box, that the game needed to end before anything else could happen. Unfortunately, given the vast amounts of controversy and pauses to the game, there was a lengthy amount of stoppage time, and time for one last incident. Alexandra Takounda slid into Houghton with enough force to send her tumbling out of play in the direction of Neville, who reacted angrily. With Houghton clutching her leg on the floor, both sets of players clashed above her as VAR was called into action once again. A yellow card rather than a red followed as the game reached a boiling point, but the final whistle blew.

England were into the World Cup quarter-finals. Yet that was somehow the least pressing matter as we left the press box for the press conference room. World Cup-winning goalkeeper Hope Solo perhaps said it best while commentating. 'I'm so glad the final whistle has been blown. We don't want to see any more injuries and I'm sick of talking about VAR.'

The discussion among journalists was a sense of disbelief at what had happened, and how both sets of managers would react, particularly with Neville seemingly sympathetic towards Cameroon and trying to calm their players down. But his demeanour changed after the late tackle to Houghton. England fans, we would later discover, had to be escorted out of the stadium by security for their own safety as tensions grew between both sets of supporters. In the post-match press conference Neville provided the quote that would splash across newspapers the following day: 'This wasn't football'.

'All the young girls watching back in England, young boys playing grassroots football, watching that kind of behaviour – I think it's pretty sad,' said Neville. 'I can't gloss over it and fudge it; I have to tell the truth … It was like when you are a kid, you lose and go home crying with the ball.'

His comments were in the heat of the moment, and while many agreed with him that the events had brought attention to the women's game for all the wrong reasons, some felt he should have acknowledged the differences in resources and preparation available between the two sides. Djeumfa, for his part, did little to acknowledge any wrongdoing. I asked the head coach whether or not he would change anything, from either his or his players' reactions if he could go back in time, and his response did little to suggest they would. 'I think we prepared to win the game and when you saw the start of the game and ultimately the game as a whole, I think we responded well. We conceded two goals but unfortunately we had a goal disallowed and if we had halved the deficit I really believe that it would have been a different result had that goal been allowed,' he said.

Both teams shared a hotel, a rare occurrence in international football, and on their return the Cameroonian staff and players are understood to have greeted the England team with a round of applause as they entered the foyer, and anger dissipated. The Confederation of African Football also offered a more balanced response the day after the match. 'Whilst remaining proud of our African teams that participated in the FIFA Women's World Cup, yesterday's match between England and Cameroon reflected badly, not only on African women's football, but African football on the whole. It is an issue which will be addressed and dealt with, at the appropriate levels of governance,' said Isha Johansen, president of the CAF women's football committee.

Among the drama and the controversy that will be remembered from 23 June 2019, perhaps its wider implications are a positive way to end, and ultimately what the World Cup journey of the Indomitable Lionesses was all about.

'Before the World Cup, not many parents would let their girls play football because it wasn't seen as something girls do,' said Nchout, who had been one of those Cameroonian players in tears on the pitch against England, a year later. 'Now lots of parents bring their girls to play football and, for me, it's a very proud moment, I'm so happy about that.'

That, ultimately, will be the legacy from the finals, rather than the memories of the battle of Valenciennes.

Afterword

Do you remember the last time? The last floodlit pitch you stood by? The last time you squeezed through a turnstile or stood in a pub to watch a game on the TV or queued outside a chip shop on the way to the stadium? The last time you watched a match before the world turned and left us here? There are millions of us who have that moment looping in our mind, reliving it as if it was both as fresh and wondrous as a newborn foal and something as old and impossible to countenance today as a black and white Pathé film reel. It was one of the reasons Steve and I wanted to put together a collection of stories about memorable football away days. To remind us, and you, of an evocative moment that we hope will one day return.

It was also something I needed to hold on to. For the best part of 15 years I've travelled to something like 90 different countries to watch football. Every one of them was wildly different yet also familiar. I still got the same excitement, that pre-match buzz where anything was possible, whether I was in Amman or Columbo or Thimphu or, as I wrote in *The Away Leg*, Pyongyang. I'm addicted to the experience and bereft without it. The moment looping in my mind is from a place just as far away and exotic as any of those cities. At least for me anyway.

Bermondsey.

It's been almost a decade since I've lived in the UK full-time, and for the past few years I've been living in Belgrade. For months I had planned a trip home to England with three Red Star Belgrade-supporting Serbian friends. It's tough for Serbs to get visas to visit the UK but after months of negotiating the Home Office's punitive bureaucracy, and securing return flights for £10, we were off to London.

Once my friends had met a Serbian contact outside Victoria to sell a few boxes of cigarettes to pay for their tickets, our next stop was the New Den to watch Millwall against Birmingham City. One of the first things I noticed living in the Balkans was the incredible popularity of *Only Fools and Horses*. My local cafe had a framed black and white picture of Del Boy and Rodney on the wall, next to counter-cultural icons like Marlene Dietrich and Leonard Cohen. Del Boy and Rodney's adventures in Peckham spoke to something important in Serbia, and elsewhere; two working-class brothers struggling for a better life in the grey economy, forces stacked against them, with both humour and pathos.

As the two were from Peckham it was obvious to almost everyone I spoke to about it that they were Millwall fans. I had tried to explain that Del Boy and Rodney's allegiances were still up for debate. The closest Del comes to full disclosure is while in a discussion with Uncle Albert in the 1990 Christmas special, 'Rodney Come Home'. Del was upbraiding Albert for not coming up with a plan to help save Rodney and Cassandra's rocky marriage. 'Well I was hoping you might come up with an idea,' he says. 'Then again I was hoping Millwall might win the UEFA Cup.'

He might have been using Millwall for comedic effect – an example of something so ridiculous that it would never, ever happen – but the club resonated with many Serbs I had met over the years. After years of war and international isolation, something chimed with Millwall's oft-quoted terrace chant, 'No one likes us, we don't care.' So Del Boy and Rodney were Millwall, and that was that.

It was the first time I had bought a ticket for a game in England for years and the experience brought back the memories of my childhood watching West

Ham United (which I kept to myself for the duration). The fear and excitement of walking from the train to the stadium. The sound of police horses clopping by. The warm flood of light as you approach the stadium. The proximity to the pitch and the greenest green, an almost Platonic green, you will ever see when you walk to your seat. The witty, responsive chants that are utterly unique to English supporter culture. The less witty philosophy of a man standing up to shout 'fuck you, you cunt' to the referee without anyone batting an eyelid. It was freezing, half-empty and ended 0-0. But that didn't matter. It was about the journey and about friendship. Del Boy and Rodney would have approved.

The next day we went to north London to watch Arsenal play Olympiacos in the Europa League. The ultras of Red Star and Olympiacos share a deep friendship, largely based on their shared Orthodox Christian faith. Before the game, in a north London pub, the large contingent of Gate 7 ultras welcomed their Serbian guests with open arms, and me with a little more suspicion.

The game ended in spectacular fashion with Youssef El Arabi scoring the winning goal in the final minute of extra time. In the packed Olympiacos away end limbs flew everywhere. But, in hindsight, that's not the most memorable moment of the night. Now, I can't escape the image of Evangelos Marinakis, the rotund owner of Olympiacos, waddling around the pitch to shake hands with the travelling support. Ten days later he was diagnosed with the novel coronavirus. For me this was the moment that a global pandemic that seemed far away arrived on our doorstep. We spent the next 24 hours drinking and laughing. And then it was all gone.

Football has endured but it is an empty experience without the fans. As I write this there is talk of a vaccine and a return to normality. It's telling that when I read the news my first thought was to consider where my first away trip would be. I would take a guess I'm far from the only person who thought that. I pray it will be that easy, and that the looping image of the last time will no longer be a full stop, but a memory superseded with the away legs to come.

James Montague, Istanbul, November 2020

About the Contributors

Nick Ames is a football journalist for *The Guardian*. He covers the Premier League on a weekly basis but likes nothing better than an old-fashioned underdog in the international game.

@NickAmes82

Martino Simcik Arese was the founder of *TIFO Magazine* and is currently editor-in-chief of COPA90 Stories. Over the past six years with the channel he has travelled to over 130 stadiums around the world to document fan culture, which is quite a long way from his first club match: LA Galaxy making their debut against the NY/NJ Metro-stars in the Rose Bowl.

@Martino_Tifo

James Corbett is a correspondent for offthepitch.com. He has authored and co-authored ten books about football, including his collaboration with Neville Southall, *The Binman Chronicles,* and *Faith of our Families,* which was longlisted in the 2018 Sports Book of the Year awards.

@james_corbett

Andrew Downie has spent most of his adult life as a foreign correspondent in Latin America, 19 years of them in Brazil. He translated the biography of Garrincha from Portuguese into English and is the author of the critically acclaimed *Doctor Socrates: Footballer, Philosopher, Legend.*

@adowniebrazil

Catherine Etoe has covered women's football for the past two decades, writing for a variety of local and national media. Her first book, *Three Lions on Her Shirt: The England Women's Story,* written with Natalia Sollohub, came out in 2007. She is also the co-author of two FIFA Women's World Cup official books. In the early 1990s she was a diligent captain, but average right-back, for Blackpool Ladies FC. She sticks to five-a-side these days.

@CatherineEtoe

Molly Hudson is a sports journalist, mainly covering football, with a specialism and passion for the growth of the women's game. She began writing for *The Times* in 2017 and has since covered the Premier League,

Champions League and Women's World Cup. She was shortlisted for Football Journalist of the Year in 2019 and won the Silver award for young sports writer at the 2020 Sports Journalism Association awards.

@M0lly_Writes

Samindra Kunti is a football journalist based in Belgium. His work features in *World Soccer, Forbes, Josimar* and *Inside World Football.* He is a regular contributor to BBC Africa. Sam is working on a book about his passion, Brazil's 1970 team.

@samindrakunti

Steve Menary has covered sport, mainly football but sometimes cricket and rugby, from Africa, the Caribbean, Europe and the Middle East and written six books, including *Outcasts! The Lands That FIFA Forgot* and *GB United? British Olympic Football and the end of the Amateur Dream.*

@MenarySteve

James Montague is a journalist and author from Chelmsford, Essex. His latest book, *1312: Among the Ultras, A Journey With the World's Most Extreme Fans*, was published by Ebury in March 2020.

@JamesPiotr

Harry Pearson is the author of 11 works of non-fiction. *The Far Corner* was runner-up for the William Hill Prize and was chosen as one of the 50 Greatest Sports Books of All Time by both *The Observer* and *The Times*. He writes a monthly column for *When Saturday Comes*, and won the 2011 MCC/Cricket Society Prize for his book about northern club cricket, *Slipless in Settle*. *Connie*, his biography of Learie Constantine, was longlisted for the 2017 William Hill Prize and won the MCC/Cricket Society Prize in 2018. His latest book, *The Farther Corner – A Sentimental Return to North-East Football*, came out in 2020.

@camsell59

Arik Rosenstein is the CEO and Founder of Passion FC, a global social movement that uses football as a means of confronting and addressing social issues. Arik has experience at the charity streetfootballworld, professional clubs Maccabi Tel Aviv and Accra Hearts of Oak, work within European fan-culture at SD Europe, and has a Sports Management degree from New York University.

@ArikRosenstein4